The

O.N.E.

Book

We Must **O**vercome Obstacles and **N**ever Give Up on
the Road to Having our Best Year **E**ver

By
Constance Carter
Tinarsha Brown
Sheila Green

First Printing, 2016

ISBN-13: 978-0-692-73623-4

Printed in the United States of America

To people who've supported us—

To the husbands and partners who've loved us—

To the angels who've watched over us—

To the mentors and advocates who've been there along the way—

And to our children, we give you a legacy of passion to chase your dreams, the promise of success, the permission to fall and to fly, and the faith to know we'll always be there to catch you.

Table of Contents

FOREWORD

O.N.E. is a must read and inspirational guide for women seeking to live their best life while managing the roles of mothers, wives and entrepreneurs. The authors Constance Carter, Tinarsha Brown and Sheila Green have walked the walk, talked the talk, and are living their dreams on a grand scale.

Hardship never stopped them for pursuing their passion, walking in their purpose and supersizing their profits. Theirs is a story of success despite the many trials and tribulations they experienced on the road to building a multi-million dollar business. As women of faith, who formed a bond of ride or die sisterhood; these remarkable women capture within these pages the good, the bad and ugly of the many obstacles that could have toppled their dreams, capsized their plans of success and caused them to simply give up.

Each of the chapters offers the reader a transparent and authentic slice of their remarkable journey in a voice that echoes and demonstrates their remarkable fortitude, grit and guts.

Never ever give-up is their mantra, hold on until the bitter gets better, and letting go of the pain are the three primary principles that each reader will see played out in these awe-inspiring stories. Holding onto the joy despite the pain, and the seemingly endless failures of financial misfortune is the stuff of champions, and this is a story about champions!

Readers, as you experience Constance, Tinarsha and Sheila, you will come to a greater understanding that being in business is a fulltime job, and it takes planning, vision and unmitigated Gaul to go the distance.

Enjoy this journey through the lens of reality, recovery and grand rewards. They did it, and so can you...

Dr. Emma Fraser Pendleton

It is your passion that empowers you to be able to do that thing you were created to do. - T.D. Jakes **#GoForIt** 🔲🔳

WELCOME TO DAY O.N.E.

Our lives ain't been no fairy tales.

It is important for us to start there because, well...it's true. We've had our share of success, both individually and as a collective. We are proud of the businesses we've created, the families we've built, and the lives we've changed. We are mothers, entrepreneurs, philanthropists, and community champions.

But our truth is we are three women who decided to fight for it.

If you picked up this book, you have something to fight for. You believe you were created for something more. And that doesn't mean you haven't strived for and already reached success in your life. Maybe you've climbed the corporate ladder, shattered the glass ceiling, and you're ready for your next professional level. Perhaps you've raised your family and now it's time to build the business you've always wanted. Regardless of where your dreams are destined to take you, you can follow our advice to get there and on your own terms. Success is a bar you get to set and define—for you. It only requires you to be authentic to who you are and committed to the process of becoming more.

When we decided to write this book, we all agreed we would do one thing—tell the truth. We wanted to be real. We wanted to be honest. We wanted to give you a glimpse of the peaks and valleys so you could see yourself in our lives, in our successes, and also in our setbacks. While it would have been easy to fill these pages with the high notes and stories all about our wins, that is not the story we desired to tell. True to who we are, this book is about as transparent as it gets. Sharing so many intimate details hasn't been easy—but nothing connected to your purpose ever is. But just like the fight for your dreams, it is necessary.

We wanted to share our stories not to cause you to question who you are or where you've been, because each of our journeys are different. But we do hope that you will see yourself in these pages, and be open to the lessons we've learned, the opportunities that await you, and the strength that undoubtedly exists in you.

Let our passion for your success leap off of these pages, become a part of you, and light your fire.

The illusion of success is a funny, sometimes deceptive, thing. We live in a world that tries to convince us every day that accolades, applause, or however you define success, comes easily. Social media and the media at large will make you believe that all you have to do is find the right gimmick, the right reality show—the right something—and it will all just magically come together. That's definitely not how it happened for us. (And we're willing to bet that's not how it happened for you either.)

Our truth—your truth—is that success is something you have to work hard for. It's something you have you have to push for. And most importantly, it's something you have to want—more than you want anything else.

Through our stories, you'll see we've had as many losses as we've had wins. We've lost homes, husbands, friends, and money. But in spite of it all, we never lost our vision. We never lost our faith. And we never gave up.

So that is exactly what this book is about. This book is about dreams. The dreams that have already been lived out and those yet to be realized. This is a book about the strength it takes to push through when the inevitable challenges come to knock you down and you have to somehow find the will to stand back up. This is a book about achieving the success you desire and about choosing faith over fear.

We hope you'll realize that if we can do it, you can do the same. Your gender doesn't matter. Your socioeconomic background doesn't matter and neither does your age. The missteps and the mistakes? They don't matter either. If it were left up to society, *all* of those things would have counted each of us out. We all beat the odds. We all survived the story. So we wrote this book to share our hard-won wisdom and our stories with you.

We didn't write this to give you the exact roadmap to launching a multi-million dollar company, although you will pick up a few tips along the way. What we know for sure is before you can reach that level of success, there is some intrinsic work you'll have to do first. Step One?

Believe.

You have to believe, down in your soul, that there is nothing that can stand between you and your destiny. You have to believe there is no goal, no dream, or no desire that is out of your reach. You have to believe you can succeed despite the odds stacked against you.

We believe you were led here because you are being called to more. So as you read and explore what's to come, think about a few questions:

What are you fighting for?

What are you willing to lay it all on the line for?

What are you willing to rise up and stand for?

What do you want to achieve—greatly?

We want you to discover those answers by the end of this book. And once you do, you will find your will. You will find your purpose. You will find the path you want to blaze.

These pages are a journey—some personal, some entrepreneurial—of what we've learned and lived. Consider them a guide, a roadmap, to help you to seek what is meaningful to you and to define success for you. It doesn't matter if your success makes sense to anyone else. Your vision doesn't require a buy-in from the world. Your dreams are for you to define. Your destiny is for you to hold. Your purpose is for you to live out. When you do each of those things, the world will be fuller, richer, and more extraordinary as a result.

But, first, you have to go for it.

This book is about finding that ONE thing that you are willing to go for, no matter what.

What is the ONE thing you want most out of this life?

What is your ONE thing you are fighting for?

What is the ONE thing you are willing to push for, press for, go beyond your limits for?

Keep that in mind as you read these words. Don't let it go.

This book is for entrepreneurs like us. It's for people—like us—who have a dream, a drive, a destiny they just can't let go of.

If you have a fire inside you that keeps you up at night because you know you were created for more—

If you want to push past your circumstances, your past struggles, and your right now—

If you want to go for it—

This book is for you.

Every obstacle is just a stepping stone to your greatness. #GoForIt

Constance Carter

Chapter 1
SOMETIMES YOU JUST GOTTA CHANGE THE TIRE

Stop Waiting.

I can't expect God to bless me with the great things if I am not willing to do the little things. - Constance Carter **#GoForIt** 🔲🔲

"This can't be for real."

There I was, on the shoulder of one of the busiest highways in the Silicon Valley. The morning rush hour was winding down and cars whizzed by me and my dusty 1980 Datsun B310 at full speed. I was headed to one of the most important job interviews of my life—a full-time, paid internship at Hewlett-Packard where I worked as a security guard. This interview was the opportunity I had worked hard and prayed harder for. I was ready.

I did everything right that morning. I got up earlier than usual. I primped, prepped, pantyhosed, and ran out of the door in enough time to arrive at my interview at least twenty minutes early. I had this internship on lock. I could feel it. All of the cards were stacked in my favor and I just needed to get to the interview so the manager and I could get on the same page. This was mine. I knew it. Soon she would too.

But instead of making my way to the office, I was sitting on the Highway 280.

With a blown tire.

I sat in the car for a few minutes to get my thoughts together and figure out a plan. Cell phone? Nope. Highway Patrolman passing by? Uh uh. Missing my interview? Hell no.

So I decided I had two options: give up and go home or go hard and change that tire. I'll give you a second to guess which route I chose.

No I wasn't going to be twenty minutes early.

But I'd be damned if I'd be late.

I flung the car door open and hopped out. The tire was on the left side closest to the oncoming traffic and it was one of the most dangerous situations a driver could be in. Not thinking twice, I popped the trunk, and lugged the spare, jack, and wrench out. Taking a deep breath, I made my way to the other side of the car.

When I purchased that car two years before, at sixteen, my father made sure I knew how to change a tire. As his instructions came flooding back to me, I had never been more grateful for him as I was in that moment. Even when he wasn't around, he didn't let me down. He was still my hero.

And in my well-pressed, grey pinstripe skirt suit, pantyhose, and heels, I changed that tire and made my daddy proud.

Five minutes before the interview was scheduled to start, I was running into the HP building. I looked every bit of the mess I had just gotten myself out of. Tire soot on my hands, stains on my suit, and holes in my hose. And to top it all off, I was a little musty. I sniffed my underarms, wet with sweat.

Umm, yes. Definitely musty.

With no time to spare, the receptionist pointed me to conference room where the hiring manager and two other managers were waiting for me. If they were shocked by my crazy appearance, they didn't let on. I played right along with them, but kept my distance—just in case the funk that held my nose somehow reached across the table.

"Do you mind if I run to the bathroom first?"

I barely waited for an answer before I bolted to the nearest ladies' room. I took off my stockings, straightened my suit, and smoothed my hair. A quick rinse of my hands and I was back in the conference room ready to get it.

Taking my seat, I felt compelled to explain everything that happened.

"You could have just rescheduled this interview. We would have understood, because it happens," the hiring manager responded when I was done with my unbelievably crazy story.

Clearly these people had never met Constance Carter.

"You don't understand. I want this job so bad and there was no way I was going miss this for anything in the world."

I walked out of there with the job.

Later that day, I called my sister to share the hilarity of everything that had happened. I was shocked when she asked the same question my interviewer had earlier. "Why didn't you just call them and tell them you couldn't come?"

That's when it dawned on me that I wasn't like everybody else. There was a distinct difference between ordinary and extraordinary, and I already knew, at eighteen years old, what side of the coin I wanted to be on. I had a drive—a fight—in me that was so natural I didn't realize it.

Soot and all.

Skirt suit and all.

Defeat isn't an option.

Just change the tire.

Extraordinary Takes Heart

My tire story is incredibly comical to me now, but I had no idea how many more "tires" I would have to change in my life. Every obstacle I have ever faced - from living in a 3 bedroom with over 20 people as an adolescent, over exposed to everything you can imagine, to my mother abandoning me when I was just 14, never looking back, to being homeless at just 18 years old - presented me with two choices:

1. Sit on the side of the road in tears.
2. Take control of the situation and work it out.

The real question?

Do you want to be ordinary or extraordinary?

In striving for success—and success means something different for all of us—we are constantly faced with the decision to settle in where we are or fight to get to where we desire to be. The former is the easiest road to travel, but is it the most rewarding? Will taking the path of least resistance lead us to where we ultimately want to be?

Choosing to press through to your purpose, even when it's hard, is what separates you from everyone else. The persistence, the insistence, to reach your goals and to get to the finish line is what distinguishes you from those who started—yet halted—in the face of failure. The determination to not allow anyone or anything to stand in your way or to stop you is a power that lies in you.

This is what makes you extraordinary.

Extraordinary is a choice.

Extraordinary takes a willingness to get dirty, to get out there, and change that tire.

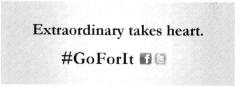

Extraordinary takes heart.

#GoForIt

Having the heart to follow your dreams means being uncomfortable. It will mean doing things you didn't think you could or would do and pushing past your comfort zone. We all have walls of comfort and security that we've built around us, and we fight to stay within them. It's safe there. It's impossible to fail there. Everything you thought you wanted is already there. Bravery not required. But a life without bravery is one without risk.

Without risk, you are not really living. And you certainly aren't moving any closer to your dreams.

Courage is something we don't have until we need it. It's when we are faced with something impossible, something we didn't think we could do—an obstacle we didn't think we could overcome—that it shows up. When you are face to face with what seems insurmountable, that is the time to test what you are really made of. All of the talk, all of the "I woulds" and all of the "I think I cans" are only a test until it's real.

Think about one thing you could do to be braver. One thing. It doesn't have to be moving a mountain or the biggest, scariest goal you have. Do you know those loud broadcast system tests that pop up on your television in the middle of the night? The network is testing their notification process for a national emergency. If something were to happen, a communication plan is in place and viewers are familiar with the signal that says, "Listen! This is what you need to do right now!"

Sometimes we need to test our courage too. If you've been in your comfort zone for a while, you may need a loud alarm in the middle of the night to wake you up. You may need a test to remind you just how powerful you really are.

You need to remember you are extraordinary!

#GoForIt 🔵🔵

Test your system today with a small win. Accomplish that and then do something else. Build on those wins for a while. Before long, you will feel your bravery start to build too. When the big test comes (and believe me, it is) you'll be ready.

If You Want Something, Go Get It. Period. - Chris Gardner
#GoForIt 🔵🔵

When Faith Goes Flat

Flat tires are like obstacles we face on the road to success. One moment you're coasting; the next you have this unexpected catastrophe on your hands. Maybe you hit a pothole and lose your job or your business is losing momentum and money as you frantically try to figure out how to stop the leak. Or someone who doesn't believe in you, your potential, or your vision, becomes a nail in the road that deflates your tire slowly. Little by little, you are doubting yourself more. You are questioning what you believed about yourself and your capacity to go get it. You don't notice you are losing air until it's too late.

And before you know it, your faith is completely flat.

With flattened faith, those once attainable goals feel impossible. The obstacles appear insurmountable. Your ability to overcome, to fight, diminishes as your self-doubt overwhelms you. Extraordinary is so far down the road, you can't even see it.

This is when your courage kicks in.

It may be buried, but it's still there. You have been brave before. You have pushed past the impossible before. You've won before.

Call on your courage to replenish your faith. Obstacles come along on your path not to threaten you, but to remind you of the strength you've placed on the shelf. Grab it and reinforce your faith with the reminder that you've conquered before and you will again.

Think about a time when you had to overcome something that seemed impossible.

Remember how powerful you felt? Did you feel like you could conquer the world after that?

The memory may have a little dust on it, but it's time to get reacquainted again. You've done some amazing things in your life. Today is the day *when you choose* to add more to that list. Find your will. Find your strength. Find your commitment to get it at all costs. Fight through the fear.

Hello, Courage. We've missed you.

Everything You Want Is On The Other Side Of Fear- Jack Canfield
#GoForIt 🔲🔲

No More Sitting On The Shoulder Of Your Dreams

When you've been knocked down enough times, finding the motivation and the momentum to get back up again is often weighted in fear. Some of us have been knocked out of the driver's seat by life's circumstances beyond our control. We've lost all control over our destinies. We've taken our hands off of the wheel. We are coasting in the ease and comfortability of lives that don't light us up or anyone else anymore.

We've started driving in the opposite direction of our purpose. Soon, we're on the side of the road, watching others' success speed by us while we wish and wait—fearful to rev up and get back out there. We don't want to take the risk.

But success says we must.

If guaranteed success was waiting for you on the other side of a busy, traffic-bustling street, would you be willing to cross? Or would the fear of the cars whizzing by keep you frozen on the sidewalk?

There were moments in my life when I hit the brakes, allowing fear to creep in and hold me still. Then I realized everything I wanted had stopped too. I decided to move. And my faith moved with me.

My hunger for my success grew to a point that I am willing to do anything to get it. *Anything.* I will face my fears. I will work harder than anyone else I know. I will sprint across the busiest freeway in the world with a baby strapped to my back to make it the other side where my dreams are waiting. Now I know that sounds a bit extreme, but it's true. The life, the success, the abundance, the greatness—is waiting on the other side. And sometimes, actually most times, you will have to be relentless and willing to do anything to reach it.

You have to hunger for it more than you fear it.

Success is an appetite. The closer you get to it, the more you want it. Once you've tasted success or even had a whiff of it, it becomes a part of you. It becomes necessary. You won't settle for anything else.

But like any appetite, success can be suppressed. Self-doubt will suppress success. Too many questions can suppress success. Fear will suppress success.

If you could snap your finger and release all fear, what would you do? What vision would change from black and white to full color? What dreams would you chase? Who would you become? Write it down.

You have everything it takes to get to the other side. You have the smarts and the strength. You have the purpose and the passion. You have the heart. It's time for you to stop watching from the side of the road and do this.

You are on the shoulder of the freeway right now. Dreams are passing by. Success is speeding by, a hundred miles per hour. The career, the life—everything you've envisioned for yourself—is on the other side. Your destiny is at stake. Now is not the time to play it safe. Now is not the time to hesitate or overthink. You have to get to the other side.

Your dreams depend on it.

Forget putting on the blinker and easing into the dream lane. Let the bumper—your faith— do its job and protect you. If your car is stalled, strap those dreams to your back, and run! How you get to the destination doesn't matter—all that matters is you get there.

No more hesitation. No more waiting for the cars to slow down or stop. Make your own lane.

Just jump out there.

Feel The Fear And Get It Anyway

So what do you do when fear stares you in the face? Here's my take on what fear really is and what you have to do to fight fear with fire.

F: You will Fail.

Failure is imminent on the road to success. The business idea may not pan out the first time around. The first time you ask for the promotion, you may be told no. Plans fall through and dreams take detours. You may fall flat on your pretty face and that's okay. Failing is inevitable and essential to your growth. Like a basic training preparing you for war, failing is just a part of your process. So don't run from it. Run to it. And always remember—it's not how you fall. It's how you get back up.

E: You will be Embarrassed.

If you ain't willing to be embarrassed, you ain't ready for success. Believe me, you will look stupid along the way. There will be people snickering and laughing at you behind your back (and maybe to your face). They will talk about you. Your job is not to listen.

When I got my real estate license, I was pumped. I didn't have the best clothes or a fancy car like some of my peers in the industry, but I was hungry. I wanted success so bad I could taste it, and I wasn't willing to allow embarrassment, shame, or anything else stand between me and it. I knew if I stayed the course, this wouldn't always be my reality.

I had a raggedy Ford Winstar and the back door would fly open whenever I turned the corner. I drove my clients around in that van like it was a brand new Mercedes sedan. I still served them and they hung right in there with me. Some of them, like The Curry's, would even hold the back door of the car for me. We were in it together.

You will look foolish and outlandish, at times. That's okay. Your opinion, your belief in you, is all that matters.

A: You have to put All of your cards on the table.

You have to be all in. Bet on yourself. Work your dream as if it's the only option in the world and nothing else matters.

No—you can't go and get a part-time job if it doesn't work.

No—you can't phone a friend to bail you out.

No—there is no Plan B and no escape route.

You're in it. Stay in it.

R: Take Risks.

Remember that image of me running across the freeway with a baby strapped to my back to my get to my dreams? Let that be you too.

Where there is risk, there is no regret. You can't live a life full of "What Ifs" or "Should Haves." When it is all said and done, you want to be able to say you tried—you did it—even if you failed.

I've made thousands of dollars taking risks and I've also lost thousands. I've made my fair share of mistakes and I accept that I will make a few more. But those losses and mistakes were worth it because I bet on me. I can look back on my life and say, "I went for it and here's what happened." When I cross the freeway, I am thinking about all of the obstacles I had to face growing up. I am thinking about the people who underestimated me. I am thinking about my husband, my kids, and their exposure to new things along with their futures. If I am too afraid to cross the street, where does that leave them? Think about who will be standing still with you before you decide to not move.

S: There will be Sleepless nights.

Successful people may not sleep regularly and they definitely don't keep normal business hours. I've traded stories with entrepreneurs from all over the world, and I can tell you that sleep is often sacrificed for success. If successful people are not thinking, planning, strategizing, or implementing, they are not moving. They are not growing.

As my business grew, I had nights when I had to stay up after my husband and kids were in bed to study, develop strategic plans, take online classes and workshops, and create infrastructures. Were there times when my pillow called? Absolutely.

But my dreams yelled louder.

Yours are calling you too.

Reasons You May Be Afraid To Trust Yourself

Here are some real reasons why you may be afraid to step out there:

- I have messed up before and I don't want to fail again. I have made too many mistakes.
- Someone in my life has told me I couldn't do anything.
- I am afraid to really put myself out there because people may criticize me.
- I feel that everyone expects me to be perfect and I don't want to let them down.
- I don't have all the answers and I can't start a business or go after the career I want until I am an expert in my industry.
- I don't want to lose my steady paycheck if I pursue my passion.
- I am scared to try something different and to step outside of my comfort zone.
- I don't want to be selfish and take time away from my children and my family to invest more time in myself.
- I am not smart or talented enough to do what I really want to do.
- I don't feel worthy of success. I haven't done anything to deserve it.

Do any of these feel familiar to you? If they do, you are not alone. We have all had moments when our fears have stepped us back and made us question ourselves and what we are capable of. But it's time to think and act differently. It's time for you to face your F.E.A.R.S, shut them down for good, and do this!

Tell yourself this:

I refuse to allow my fears to hold me back from pursuing my dreams. I used to be afraid of:

_____

_____

_____

_____

_____

But I am not anymore. I am moving past my fears and committing to boldness, bravery, and a life full of passion and the fulfillment of my goals.

I want it more than I am afraid of it.

Chapter 2
PLAY ANYWAY

There's No Time to Wait for Anyone Else.

It's your road, and yours alone. Others may walk it with you but no one can walk it for you. – *Rumi* **#GoForIt** ▪️▪️

Believe in yourself.

There is not a person alive who hasn't heard this phrase more times than they can count. Any motivational message or speech we've ever heard tells us this is something we need to do. According to what we read, hear, and see, our lives, our success—anything we want to do in this life—hinges on our ability to figure out this self-love thing and truly believe in ourselves.

So we spend our lives looking for a source, something or someone we can grab, hold on to, and fill our spirits with the self-esteem—the belief—we need.

We might read a few inspirational books.

Repeat some affirmations.

Pray. (With no action—we'll talk about that another time).

We search. We seek. We exhaust ourselves trying to find the thing everywhere else that really lies with us.

I have a question for you: Are you tired yet?

The truth is belief in ourselves is not an external thing. Now we can, if we're lucky, have someone in our lives who can boost our self-esteem, cheer us across the finish line, or plant a seed in our minds that helps us formulate a strong sense of self. But what happens when that person doesn't exist? What happens when we look over our shoulder and there is no one there to pat our backs? What happens when we're faced with an obstacle to overcome or an opportunity to do something great and we're alone?

You play anyway.

That's because believing in yourself is all about who you are. It's about having an internal faith that you sustain, one that isn't dependent on what anyone else says, thinks, or does. It's yours.

You can't borrow belief. You've got to claim it. You've got to own it.

Because sometimes, it just going to be you and God.

We all have this vision of an entire team running beside us. We want our families there. We want our friends there. We want our peers and colleagues with us, tooting horns, beating drums, and cheering us on. That would be wonderful. But if it doesn't happen, if there is no one else there but you, will you push anyway? Will you dream anyway? Will you move anyway?

Can you tell yourself, "I can do this?"

You will never rise above the level at which you see yourself- Constance Carter
#GoForIt 🔲🔲

Be Your Own Cheerleader

When we envision a cheerleader, an image of a cute, happy chick with Pom Poms and a big smile comes to mind, right? Besides being cute, a cheerleader's job is to come out on to the court or the field and to get the crowd and the players hype. Sure, she dances, performs, and makes sure everyone in the building is excited and has a great time. But a cheerleader can't show a player how to make the shot or run the touchdown. A cheerleader can't instill that fiery will or that get-up-and-get-it strength needed to win the game. She's not supposed to. It's not her job.

After she walks back to the sideline, she's done what she came to do. Now it's time for the players to do the same.

Your life is no different.

There will be times when you'll have to push yourself. There will be times when no one else sees the dream or the vision the way you do, if they see it at all. There will be times when you expected someone to show up for you, but you'll look around and they won't be there.

When it's time to play in this life, you may have to be your own cheerleader.

#GoForIt

Play anyway.

Trust me, for your destiny, it's so worth it.

Growing up, my father was my hero. He was my Superman. My encourager. And I did everything to live up to his expectations of me. I refused to let him down. Daddy said I was smart, so I excelled in school. I got the grades and played every instrument I could get my hands on. He said I was a leader, so I was always in the front of the class.

And he was always on the front row—be it of a concert or my life—cheering me on.

I remember my final high school band concert. It was such a big night for me. This concert meant everything, not only because it was the last time I'd take the stage at that school, but it was a culmination of everything I'd worked so hard for. I loved music and I'd mastered every instrument I played. That night, I was going to give a show—drums, cello, bass, the upright bass, and the percussions. I just knew my dad would be there, on the front row, listening to every note I played. I watched the door the entire night, waiting for my father to walk though.

He never did.

I learned later that he was with his new girlfriend and chose to spend time with her instead of coming to watch my performance. I had always been his Number One girl and he was always my hero, my staple, the constant in my life. Now all of that had changed.

When he got married a few months later, things really took a turn for the worse—at least for me. He asked me to leave our home, and just like that, I was homeless. I bounced from house to house, couch to bed, sleeping anywhere I could lay my head for the night, - sometimes in that old Datsun B310.

I'd grown up with almost nothing, so I was used to losing or never having lots of material things, or even full meals for a lot of my childhood. This was different though. I was a young adult woman now, and the childlike everything's-gonna-be-alright outlook was gone, at least in that moment. I didn't have much as a little girl, but my dad had been there. The words he'd always told me, "You are going to be the President of the United States," had been there. My mother telling me how smart I was had been there. The reminder from my Sunday School teacher that I was just as important as anyone else had been there. Those words were still a part of me, but I'd never felt like this before. I felt abandoned. Lost. Unsure of what do next.

I was all grown up now—on my own—whether I wanted to be or not.

Work Harder, Run Faster, Jump Higher, Go Further

Season after season, experience to experience, my belief in myself was tested. Before I ventured into real estate, I worked in marketing and logistics for HP. I loved my job, and I was good. I knew as a woman, and particularly as a black woman, I couldn't afford to slip. I had to work harder, run faster, jump higher, and go further than anyone else. My department applauded my work. I received countless outstanding reviews and praise. Yet, none it was acknowledged by the older, white men who ran our department. I could feel their disdain for me every time I walked in the room. They looked down on me and, at every opportunity, tried to make me feel less than who I knew I was. It didn't matter how incredible I was. It didn't matter how well I spoke or how great I was at my job.

All they saw was a twenty-something black girl.

But all I saw was that little girl who could be anything she wanted to be.

The point of my story is that you have to believe in yourself, who you are, and what you are here to do. People and circumstances will test you and everything you've ever thought about yourself. Maybe you've always had a strong sense of self and maybe you are still trying to find that place. But here's what I want you to know...

You are just as important as anyone else.

I've lived by those eight words all of my life. And now, I want to leave them with you. Believe you can have it all. Believe you belong in any space and any place you walk into—because you do. Believe that no one has the right to stand between you and your destiny. Because they don't.

When I shared my desire to open my own real estate company with my father for the first time, I expected him to be as elated as I was. I knew I was ready to do it, and while I didn't have every detail worked out yet, I had the vision. And I thought I would have the support from everyone who loved me.

It didn't happen.

"You can't do it because you're black and you're a woman."

I heard those words come out of my father's mouth, and I was immediately thrust into a scene from, *The Color Purple*. *Did he really just say what I think he said? Was this not the 21st century? Were there not women around me doing everything I was setting out to do and more?*

My pride took a quick step back. His words stung. I never thought in a million years that my father would doubt me or question my capabilities. This was someone who had always told me I could be anything and do anything. Was I hurt? Yes.

Would I stop?

No.

We've all had people come along who aren't as inspired or invested in our dreams as we are. But this is why God gave you the vision and not them. When people doubt you, it doesn't mean stop—it means prove them wrong. You *will* have to put in more work. You *will* have to outrun and outjump those next to you. You *will* have to go further than everyone else.

This is the moment you were built for. You thought the negativity came to tear you down, but it was really to build you up. All of the people who didn't believe in you, well, they had a purpose too—to remind you of what you were really created for.

Who has ever underestimated you or counted you out? Did you believe them? Clear your heart, mind, and spirit of those negative thoughts and beliefs. You can't allow anyone else to crush your dreams.

You've blocked the negative noise. You have a goal and you're set on it. You're determined to make it happen, no matter what. You've claimed it.

That's just the first few steps. Let's get ready for what's next.

Anything you want in this life that's worth anything, you will have to fight for it. Nobody is going to stand in line to hand you a basket of dreams. I've failed, I've filed bankruptcy, and I've been willing to look like a fool to the world, to be embarrassed, all in the name of chasing my success. I want you to be willing to do the same.

You have to be willing to go in. You have to be willing to push when it's hard.

You have to go get it.

So...

If no one has ever told you that you can be anything you want to be, please let me be the first.

If no one has ever been on the front row of your life, clapping and cheering you on, *you* be the first.

If someone was there for a part of your life, and they're not right now...well, maybe that season has passed.

When it comes to your destiny—the thing that God is calling you to do—you have to choose. There is something in this life that you were purposed to do, and like it not, it's your choice to claim what already belongs to you, what's rightfully yours.

Your gender—it doesn't matter. The color of your skin, where you were born, where you went to school or even if you didn't, none of that can hold you back. You have been equipped to accomplish anything you want. You can have it all. Regardless of who says otherwise.

I want you to do something. Get up and go look in the mirror. Stand there for a minute and take a good look at yourself.

Do you see that reflection staring back at you?

That person—*right there*—is everything you need. Stop telling yourself you aren't enough. Stop questioning whether you have enough.

Do you believe in yourself enough to rise higher?

Good.

Now go soar.

Chapter 3

BE WILLING TO PUT ALL OF YOUR CARDS ON THE TABLE

Bet on you.

God has an interesting way of pushing us towards the destiny He's defined for us.

Sometimes we see the signs, the writing on the wall, and we move without hesitation or question.

And, sometimes, it takes a little more effort on His part. We ignore the nudges, the confirmations, even the "messengers" who come our way. (Every once in a while somebody has a word for you that is *really* from Him and not them. I am sure you know what I mean.) So our safety net gets yanked away and before we know it, we're in the middle of the ocean—our assignment—doggie paddling like our lives depend on it, trying to keep our heads above water.

Lifejacket TBD.

Like so many people, my safety net used to be a full-time job in Corporate America. Actually, make that *two* jobs, thanks to my husband's career. In 2002, I was doing very well in IT at Cisco Systems. I'd been with the company for a few years after leaving HP and the position and salary were ideal, offering us the flexibility and financial stability we needed for our young family. Things were going really well for us—until they weren't. The dot.com bubble burst and my nice every-two-week paycheck would soon be replaced with a pink slip, a lump sum severance, and a goodbye lunch.

After the initial shock wore off, it dawned on me that the layoff was really a blessing in disguise. I'd started dabbling in real estate and was quickly falling in love with the industry. I was fascinated with housing, how transactions worked, and most importantly, helping people by connecting them to the information and resources they needed to make informed buying decisions. The more I learned, the more I shared. Soon, I was the go-to girl for all things real estate for family and friends. For me, it was about more than buying a house—it was about building wealth. I knew I wanted my real estate license eventually. The layoff was just the push I needed.

What looked like an obstacle to some was really an opportunity for me. Real estate was what my heart longed to do. It had become my passion and, finally, this was something I could pour my soul into. Now was my chance to build a dream for myself and my family, as opposed to helping some company build theirs. The security of a job had held me back, but now I had no choice but to jump in with both feet. The safety net was gone. No fins, no inflatable swim ring around my waist—nothing. It was time for the deep end of the pool – I had to bet on me.

It's moments like these that show us what we're really made of and who we really are. In what felt like an instant, my entire life had shifted and I had two choices—drown and die or fight like hell to keep my head above water. That innate desire in me to fight only grew stronger and bolder now that I was faced with yet another obstacle in my life that threated to take me under if I were willing to allow it. This truly felt like a life or death situation for me, leaving me no choice but to put it all on the line.

I wanted success as much as I wanted to live. – Constance Carter
#GoForIt

This was it.

My husband and I decided I would take my nice severance package and go for my real estate license. He made a great salary, so he would cover us while I built my business. With more time to fully focus on studying and a renewed sense of determination, I knew I could really go hard. I still had a few months before Cisco let me go, so we had it all planned out. More than just the money, leaving my two-hour commute behind would be the icing on the cake. I could actually see the house I was paying for and spend more time with our new baby. This was the moment I'd been waiting for. My husband had my back, supporting me, and that was all I needed.

I came home after my last day, exhausted but exhilarated at the same time. I'd spent my last evening on the highway traveling from work to home and I couldn't wait to start the next chapter of my life. I felt alive, free, and ready. I walked in the door prepared to share my excitement with my husband.

"Honey, I'm ready. We're gonna do this…"

The look on his face stopped me mid-sentence. He didn't have to say a word for me to know something wasn't right. In fact, something had to be really wrong.

"I got laid off from my job too."

Mortgage. New Baby. A few weeks' worth of severance. And a soon-to-be-up-and-coming real estate business that could take months, maybe a year, to really start bringing in the money I knew I could make.

Lifejacket, please.

If there ever was a moment to be *slightly* (okay, really) concerned, this would have been it. The real estate business was my dream and

I had every reason to believe it would successful. But now I had to think about our family and how to start bringing money in before I had a solid plan to earn a single dollar as an agent. *How long would it take to start bringing the money in? Could we really afford to do this?* All of these thoughts are dancing around in my head, adding and subtracting our present and our future to make sense of everything that was going on. While I was worrying, my husband had already made the decision on our next move.

"I'm gonna do whatever I have to do to support you."

And he did. He took the first job he could get, paying minimum wage, so I could go after my dreams. We were both committed to making it happen, but the stretch and the stress of it would at times come down on us like an emotional ton of bricks. My husband's income barely covered our expenses and my account with my severance was thinning out by the second.

Every penny he made went back into the household and I had to find the money in our nonexistent budget to attend training classes, print flyers, and keep gas in the car to show homes all evening and on the weekends. It was scary to not know how we would cover the bills from one month to the next. Sometimes there was enough—more times there wasn't. Still, I held on to the promise that at some point, there would be. For now, my only choice was to do everything I could to make this work. I didn't know what our Plan B was. Actually, I take that back. I did know.

It was Plan A.

___

What is your Plan A? You don't have to map out your entire business plan right now, but start to sketch it out. Say it so you can feel it. See it so you can do it.

___

If you are willing to do what's easy, life will be hard. But if you are willing to do what's hard, life will be easy. - T. Harv Ecker

#GoForIt 🔲🔲

I knew we didn't have anything else to fall back on but each other and this dream I had to build my business. We put all of our cards on the table and bet on us. We were sacrificing so much to make this work. We fell behind on our mortgage and almost lost our home. The bank account went in the red. We lived a no-frills lifestyle—no movies, no shopping, no vacations. But my determination to win, at all costs, grew alongside the pile of overdue bills that flooded our mailbox. Going back to corporate wasn't an option, so I had to do whatever it took. I gave myself a year to make it happen. Within six months, I'd made $75,000 and matched my Cisco salary.

I've never made anything under six figures in my business since.

Betting on myself was the most important decision I had to make.

You can only become truly accomplished at something you love. Don't make money your goal. Instead, pursue the things you love doing, and do them so well that people can't take their eyes off you. – Maya Angelou

#GoForIt 🔲🔲

Purpose Leads, Passion Follows

Never underestimate the power of passion. I could attribute my success to a number of things, including working hard (in fact, my personal tagline is Nobody Works Harder than Constance Carter!) and praying harder. Both of those are at the top of my list. But the passion that God has placed in me to go after my dreams and build a business that makes such a significant difference in people's lives is also what carried me through those moments of negative bank accounts, sinking credit scores, and all that tossing and turning with a mind full of "What's around the corner, God?" thoughts at night.

Grab your lifejacket and jump in that ocean. Swim against the current. I promise you'll make it.

Remember, no (huge) risk, no reward.

It's the passion that will hold you and affirm for you that betting on yourself is worth every bit of the risk.

#GoForIt 🔵🔵

In 2006, I felt it was time to grow again. I'd been very successful with the brokerage I was working with, but there was something missing for me. I'd become an agent because my husband and I had such a horrible experience with our buying our first home, and I'd entered the industry to make more of a difference than a dollar. The more time I spent actually working as an agent as opposed to looking in from the outside, I was more convinced that I wanted a different type of business. I wanted to help people, to be more about transforming lives and less about the transaction. But I didn't have a desire to go out on my own—at least not yet.

Still trying to piece it all together, I decided to get my broker's license. Honestly, I didn't think I'd ever use or need it. Despite my desire to open my own brokerage, the idea of doing it still wasn't on my mind. I just wanted to expand my skills and deepen my knowledge on the transaction side. Couldn't hurt.

There was God again with the nudge. He knew exactly what was around the corner. I just needed to make the turn. Eight months pregnant, I studied for the test, waddled into the testing center a few weeks later, and passed. I still sold real estate for a few years, but I had my license tucked away for a rainy day.

By 2010, I was sitting in my own office.

And the sign on the door read *Constance Carter, CEO, Catalyst Real Estate Professionals.*

I followed my passion to serve people and to transform lives through real estate. I followed my passion to create wealth for families and their future generations. I followed my passion and took a major step towards my purpose.

Here's the thing about our purpose. The path is not always clear. You won't always know what's next. All you can do is put one foot in front of the other. If it *feels* right, chances are it is. Trust your instincts. Trust the passion that has been planted in you. Passion is your guide. If you love it, chances are you are in the right place or at least moving in the right direction.

Stay true to your vision for your future. Love your work and what you put out into the world. Allow your passion to align with your purpose.

What Are You Holding In Your Hand?

Imagine you have playing cards in your hand. Each one of them represents something important in your life—your purpose, your dream, your idea, support from people around you, and even God. This is your deck, the hand you chose to play with. You are already holding everything you need to start moving.

Collect more cards as you need them along the way. You will pick up more knowledge, more resources, more people to build your dream with you. The deck will be there. Choose the cards you need.

So what do you leave out of your hand? Fear. Doubt. Excuses. None of these negative thoughts have any place in your winning hand. When you pick those cards up, toss them out immediately. You don't need them. Period.

You've been dealt a beautiful hand. In your hand, you have the faith source you need, the push-though-to-get-through you need, and the passion you need. You've counted your cards enough.

Now it's time to place your bet to win. On you.

Risk It All To Gain It All

Putting all of your cards on the table requires a blind type of faith and a willingness to push past fear. Your hand could include your job, a steady paycheck, and a nice, comfortable life. Now, don't get me wrong, I am not saying you shouldn't have all of that—and more if you desire—but my guess is if you are reading this book, you suspect (like I do) that there is something else for you to do. That's the thing I want you thinking about.

The question you have to ask yourself is, What is the jackpot?

What do you stand to win?

That is what you need to risk it all to gain it all for.

And let me say this—as women we often feel we have to lose something significant so we can gain more. More money means longer hours and less time with our families. More time spent investing in ourselves and our dreams means we can't be everything to everybody anymore. Yes, that is true. But you will be there for the people who matter most.

You get to define what it all means to you. And whatever that it is, you can have it. Family, love, passion, success—you claim it and it's yours.

You don't have to sacrifice anything you love for your success. In fact, you only become more. Because of my career, my children have more, not less. I am able to spend more quality time with them and expose them to new, exciting things that I wouldn't be able to if I had given up on what I wanted.

Betting *on* me was betting *for* them.

If it's a better future for your family and your children, bet on it. If it's a dream of owning your business or maybe a promotion, bet on it. If it's taking control of your health and starting to work out regularly, bet on that too.

Whatever you want, it's worth it.

Success leaves clues. – Tony Robbins **#GoForIt** 🔲🔲

The Bet To Win Blueprint

If you study any successful person's journey, you are likely to find a consistent pattern. The pattern is a roadmap, a blueprint, which has guided their path to greatness. Be it biblical principles or laws of the universe, these same steps will yield success for you.

1. **Visualize It.** The first step to accomplishing a goal is to have one. Think about what you want to do. Try to be as clear as possible. Proverbs 29:18 says, "Where there is no vision, the people perish." Success is impossible without a vison.

2. **Write It.** There is something very powerful about writing down your goals. Once you've determined what your goal is, put together your to-do list. Work your plan and watch those things come into fruition. Habakkuk 2:2 tells us, "Write down the vision and make it plain."

3. **Speak It.** Your goals should become your affirmations—so say them out loud every day. Keep them close and in front of you in your car, on your desk, and your phone. Summon your life, success, health, and wealth into existence. When you put your words into the Universe, an energy begins to move in the atmosphere. Every morning before I got to the gym, I pull up my goals and read them out loud. I can feel things beginning to shift in my favor and I am reminded of specific tasks I need to complete to reach my goals that day.

4. **Embody It.** Faith without works is dead. Thinking, writing, and speaking are great and they are the vehicle to point you to your destiny. But embodying is the fuel to actually get you there. Whatever your goal is, you need to eat, drink, sleep, breathe, and live it. If you need to invest, do it. If you need a degree, take classes. Study free information on the Internet, listen to audio books if you don't have time to read, network and meet as many people in your industry as you can (and don't forget to follow up with them). Take massive action NOW!

If you follow these four steps, you will manifest what you desire. Manifestation is the fruit of your labor. It's the harvest of the success seeds you've planted.

Sow and then reap.

ONE MORE THING...

Every Obstacle Is An Opportunity.

Learning to see your obstacles as opportunities takes conscious effort. We are groomed to see challenges as setbacks and as reasons (and often excuses, if we are honest) to permanently pause.

I want you to start to see your obstacles differently. I want you to stop focusing so much on what went wrong. Instead, laser in on the most important part— how to turn it around.

Obstacles come to build you and not break you. Obstacles give you clarity and show you where you can be better. Obstacles are always opportunities to grow. So don't run from your challenges. Embrace them. Allow them to become your best teacher.

Believe me, there are no better lessons *in life.*

Ten Traits of a Go-Getter

1.   Be Grateful: Acknowledge your journey for what is. Your life and your lessons are what made you who you are. Be grateful for everything you have while striving for more.

2.   Be Accepting: See the beauty and grace in others around you. We all have something to learn from one another, so be open to meeting and connecting with new people.

3.   Be Confident: You get to decide how you see you—no one else. Love yourself the way God loves and know you deserve everything this universe has to offer.

4.   Be Positive: Maintaining a positive mindset is essential. Stay on the bright side of things. Expect great things to happen. And find renewal sources for your faith, physical, and

spiritual strength such as prayer, meditation, or a challenging workout.

5.   Be Passionate: Allow your passion to fuel your purpose. You will always give your all to the one thing you are most passionate about.

6.   Be Brave: Be bold at all costs. Go for your dreams, even when they seem far-fetched. Don't allow fear to hold you hostage to a mediocre life.

7.   Be Relentless: Today's no is tomorrow's yes. N.O. simply means Next Opportunity. If there is something you want, go after it. Fearlessly.

8.   Be Extraordinary: Always go above and beyond without needing to be asked. Set the bar high for yourself and for others. Do more than what is necessary. Give more. Do more. Be more.

9.   Be Strong: Don't falter when times are tough. Stick it out. Persevere. Build an endurance—an unshakable faith—to see you through the valleys.

10.   Be a Leader: You can't lead from the back. Step up to the front of the room and own it.

Two things you never get to do —

quit and give up. #GoForIt 🄵🄶

Tinarsha Brown

Chapter 4

BEHIND CLOSED DOORS

Close one door and open another.

From the age of five until I turned eleven years old, I decided to stop talking.

Now for a kid who loved talking more than life itself, that was pretty serious. If you were to ask any of my teachers what they remember most about me, chances are they would say my mouth. I was never at a loss for words, even as a little girl, and talking in class always led me to trouble. My voice was lost at home, so school was the one place I felt safe and empowered enough to speak—and assured someone would actually listen.

My father loves to tell the story of one of the many times I got caught in class doing what I did best. One of my teachers must have called Daddy before I got home, because when I walked through the door, he was on it. He towered over me, demanding an explanation, and I had to come up with something—fast. I quickly rationalized my response in my seven-year-old mind and decided lying probably wasn't the best idea. So the only option was to tell my truth.

"I don't know, Daddy," I told him with a straight face. "My mouth just keeps moving by itself."

You can't knock a girl for trying, right?

I grew up in an abusive home where the less I spoke, the safer I felt. My father physically abused my mother until the day she left him. A compulsive gambler, he would risk it all to win it all—but more often than not, he lost. We were evicted more times than I can count, and we lived in the uncertainty of loss, never knowing when we'd come home and find what was left of our things tossed all over the street in front of the house we temporarily called home.

Daddy's disappointment, the shame of letting down his family, and his own mental demons would show up as abuse. My mother bore the brunt of it, and when I cried or tried to help her, he would turn his anger to me. At some point I made the connection that if I spoke, bad things would happen to me.

If he can't hear or see you, he can't hurt you.

So I hid. In silence.

****

We'd been evicted and we were staying with my grandmother. In my eight-year-old eyes, her house was huge, and even though she didn't have much, I remember running from room to room, playing hide-and-seek. My father was playing with me, and it was so rare to find him actually in a good, playful mood. I giggled as I ran into one of the bedrooms and hid behind the door. I heard my father counting down from the stairs below. My heart was beating a million miles a minute as I crouched down, still. Behind that door, I knew he wouldn't find me. I was safe there.

I'm winning.

"Tinarsha! Tinarsha, come out here!" He called my name over and over again, but I didn't move. When he finally grew tired of playing, he called my name again, this time with that tone that only a parent can produce. I knew then that we weren't playing anymore. The game was over. And the daddy that I knew was back.

Reluctantly, I came from behind the door and he was in my face in a flash. "Didn't you hear me tell you to come out?" he yelled.

"But we were playing a game. I was winning." The fear in me began to swell as I'd seen him angry like this before. I knew he was about to flip and there was no door for me to run to.

He turned and walked over to a lamp that sat on a nearby table. Picking up a napkin, he unscrewed the hot bulb from the lamp and with it in hand, he stormed toward me. Snatching my arm with one hand, he turned my hand upward and pressed the bulb into my skin. I cried out so loud in pain. My mother and grandmother came rushing into the room to assist, not knowing what was going on. It was too late; the harm was done. I didn't move until he dropped the napkin and walked away.

I still have that scar on my wrist today.

Don't give up. Normally it is the last key on the ring which opens the door. –
Paulo Coelho **#GoForIt** 🔲🔲

Doors To Dreams

Behind every closed door you've faced, or are facing right now, something you need awaits you. It could be a new idea, a new dream, or a new vision. It could be the last piece of information or a resource you need to finish that business plan. It could be the final piece to your puzzle—the one you've been waiting to find.

When we hesitate to open the doors in front of us, we delay our dreams. If we don't push, we'll never get to the purpose. We'll never reach our big goals and we'll never grab hold of the success that may feel beyond our reach, but it's really *right there*. We'll never have the passion-filled careers and businesses we've dreamed of. We'll never become the people we were born to be.

> **The doors to our dreams are to be opened. Try the key. Turn the knob. Knock. Find out what's waiting for you.**
>
> **#GoForIt**

If you encounter a door that won't budge, regardless of how hard you push, take a step back. Is this protection? Is this someone you have been pushing and pressing to come along with you, to believe in you and to support you, but they just won't get on board? Is this door closed for a reason?

What is standing between you and your dreams? Is it negative self-talk? *Is it another person?* Remember, *never let someone else determine your worth.* Their can't doesn't have to be yours. You can.

Leave those doors that hold the naysayers closed. Turn around. Get out of those rooms of negativity and discouragement. There are so many more doors waiting for you and you have an entire house of aspirations and desires to explore. Those are the doors to your dreams and the promise of purpose God has for you. Don't give up.

For every door to your dreams, there is a key to open it. Let's talk about those keys for a minute.

Key #1: Faith

If you want to open the doors to your dreams, you have to have faith. Even when you don't have money, support, or a clear path towards your purpose, faith will carry you. Faith is a reminder that, in the end, your promise will be fulfilled. Faith is assurance. Faith is power. Keep it with you—always.

Key #2: Passion

Like faith, passion carries you through those tough times. On your road to success, there will be those, "What have I gotten myself into?" moments. You will want to close the door and run back to that job, that security, and that place where you can be safe. But that's when you grab hold of that passion. Your passion is your why, your meaning, your reason to keep going. Your passion is your heartbeat and your breath in those moments—those seasons—when the dream feels too big. Passion grows in the presence of other passionate people. The more you're exposed to it—surrounded by it—the more you'll be able to build your own. Find your passion—it will see you through.

Key #3: Goals

You can't get to a destination if you have no idea where you are going. When you get to a door of resistance, check your push against your goals. What are you setting out to do? What are you going for? Your goals are your roadmap. Make the decision about which doors to open based on your goals.

Today, there are doors that are beckoning you to turn the knob and come inside. What are you waiting for? Move towards those doors. A little closer. Now, a little closer. Go in. Your dreams are waiting. One door leads to another. One dream leads to another.

Keep turning knobs. Keep trying keys.

Opening My Own Doors

While doors protected me often as a little girl, as a woman, they took on new meaning.

Whenever I turned a corner, there was a new door—something or someone that stood between me and a goal or what I wanted. That once-silent and shy child became a strong-willed woman who when faced with a door, decided she had two choices—hide behind it or break it down.

I always chose the latter.

Real estate proved to be no exception.

I wasn't attracted to the idea of becoming a real estate agent at all. By my twenties, my mother had established a very lucrative career in the industry and earned multiple six-figures over the course of it. After graduating from college, I worked in Silicon Valley and assisted her with transactions in the evenings. She did everything she could to encourage me to get my license, and I resisted. Through my mom's lens, the sales side of real estate just didn't seem exciting to me. Running indecisive clients around from house to house to house. Wasting gas. Listening to their endless complaints. Babysitting their cats (Hey, you'd be surprised what crazy stuff people ask you to do). None of it was appealing. Not even for those huge commission checks. My sanity was worth a lot more. I was a newly divorced mother of two small boys, and my focus was on a steady check and being there to take care of them. I had more than enough on my plate. Give me my money and let me go.

Things changed when, a few years later, I met my now husband. We decided to purchase our first home together, and after denying me a chunk of the commission from the sale (I really did most of the work), my mother finally won. I got my license in 2002 and I was ready to hit the ground running.

I am a learner at heart, so I registered for a realtor's boot camp in San Jose, California. I knew some heavy-hitters in the industry would be there, so as a tenacious newbie, I was excited. I couldn't wait to get in that room.

On the morning of the event, I walk in and it's packed. There are at least 200 other people in the audience, all of us anxious to learn something that would take our careers and our bank accounts to the next level. The event featured a panel of successful brokers and agents from all over the country, so if you needed answers, these were the people you wanted to ask.

Finally, the time came for questions from the attendees and I didn't think twice before I jumped to my feet. This was the perfect opportunity to get some insight from people I respected, and I am sure there was a part of me that sought a bit of validation too. I wanted to wow the room and get these panelists to recognize me as the rising star I was.

I stepped up to the microphone and in my best, bright-bubbly-twenty-something-the-world-can't-stop-me voice, I introduced myself. "Hi, I'm Tinarsha Brown, and I am starting as a part-time agent. What is it going to take for me to be successful in this business?" I smiled and waited patiently for the warm hello, million-dollar advice, and an invitation to call somebody's office after the conference. What I got was just the opposite.

The first panelist, a man, leaned in to the microphone in front of him.

"You'll never be successful. I don't hire part-time agents. "

I felt small enough to shrink into the floor.

The second panelist was a woman, so surely she would have my back. She had someone's back alright. But it wasn't mine. Echoing the sentiments of her peer, she also affirmed the belief that I wouldn't make it.

I shrunk even deeper into the floor.

One by one, all four of other panelists weighed in with a similar response. I nodded and walked back to my seat. Inside I could feel that all-too-familiar fire and fight rising up in me.

This was just another door.

On Mother's Day of that same year, I held my first open house. By July, I'd become Rookie of the Year for my brokerage. And the wins kept coming. Before I knew it, I was earning enough to leave my job and run my real estate business full-time. I never looked back.

The following year, I ran into that same male panelist from the conference. I walked into his brokerage to handle a transaction with another agent, and when I realized it was his office, I knew I couldn't let this pass. This was my very own when-Julia-Roberts-goes-back-to-stunt-on-those-sales-women-in-the-bougie-boutique moment. Truly full-circle.

Thank you, God. Only He could orchestrate a beautiful situation like this.

Smiling to myself, I walked into his office. He snaps his head up and stares at me without saying a word.

"Hello, I'm Tinarsha Brown. Do you remember me?"

"No."

Maybe he didn't. But my spirit tells me he knew my face, but was unwilling to give me the satisfaction of acknowledging it. Unbothered, I continued with my mission. "Well, I just wanted to stop in and thank you."

A look of confusion crossed his face. *Perfect.*

"Thank you for giving me the push I needed. "

"How did I do that?"

"You told me I would never be successful. Well I am."

And with that, I turned and sauntered right on out of there.

My grandma would call that nice-nasty.

Sometimes, you just gotta let 'em know.

They Will Try To Close The Door On You

There will always be someone, somewhere, trying to close a door on you. The person who will tell you "you aren't smart or skilled enough to start a business." The husband who leaves you with two young children to raise on your own. The boss who tells you haven't done enough to earn that raise or promotion.

Those people have made up their mind about who you are and what you are destined to be. They've decided what your capabilities are, determined you are limited—stuck—right where you are. They have thrown up a door that won't budge.

You are face to face with resistance. So you have a choice to make.

Will you hide behind it or will you break it down?

At every turn, there will be someone waiting to convince you to give up. Sometimes their doubt stems from their own fears and their own failures. Misery loves company. The unambitious do too.

These are your dreams, your goals, and your destiny. Nobody else's. So you have to be emphatic about your own success. Doing so means you may not be as popular or liked. You may not be considered as nice. But you will be known as the person who didn't give up. You will be known as the person who, despite those who tried to hold you back, went for it. You will be known as the person who beat the odds.

Which would you rather be?

Doors You Need To Break Down Today

I'd love to tell you that every door I've faced has been someone else's doing. Yes there have been a fair share of those, but the truth is, there were some I created for myself. Winning the game often means we have to face our own fears, our own demons, and bottom line, get out of our own way.

Are you willing to fight for it—even if it means you're the person you need to push past to do it?

Door #1: Self-Doubt

We can be our own worst enemies. We talk ourselves out of the success we deserve before we can get one foot in. Stop it! You can push through that door. Stand firm. Work hard. Apply yourself. You can have anything in this world you are willing to work hard for.

When that man told me I wouldn't be successful as an agent, I could have allowed those seeds of doubt to grow and keep me from watering my dreams. But I didn't. I knew the best thing I could do for them, and anyone else who doubted me, was to win.

When you give up, *they win*.

When you push through, *you win*.

Allow your self-doubt to push you and not pause you. You can do it.

Get out of your own head. And get out of your own way.

Door #2: Comparison

Have you ever heard the saying, "Comparison is the thief of joy"? It's so true. We live in a world where comparing ourselves to other people is so easy. There was a time when you were only captivated by a celebrity's seemingly better life when you turned on the television—with social media, it's the girl next door. We are constantly questioning whether or not we're good enough and wondering why our grass isn't as green as the next woman's.

So here's what I want you to do: stay away from Facebook, worrying about what so-and-so is doing, did, and said. Direct that energy toward your goals and the things you set out to achieve.

She is not your competition—you are. I wake up every day motivated to beat the only person who matters. Me.

I want you to do the same.

Door #3: Giving Up Too Soon

Studies show that only 8% of people who set goals actually achieve them. I am just going to set that right here.

My point is it's so much easier to quit.

I am often asked how I stay so focused on my goals. I've developed a level of focus and discipline that is unshakable. Even when I want to quit, I can't. It's all in my mind. I am out of my bed by 5:00 am every day, at the gym a few minutes later, and then back home or to my office to start my day before 7:00 am when most people are just rolling over to check Instagram. I don't tell you this to brag, but to make the point that when you stay firm in your decision to be your best, the rest becomes easy.

When we sit down with our to-do lists every day, we tend to tackle the easiest things first. Accomplishing those things are great (it's better than not doing anything at all), but those teeny goals are often distractions from doing the stuff we really need to do, but are afraid to face. You convince yourself that they're not achievable, so you go after the little things to make yourself feel accomplished.

From now on, big things first. Get to the hardest, most challenging items on your list first. Knock those out and then come back to the other things if there time left in your day. Stop playing.

Dust Yourself Off And Try Again

Simply put—you will fall and you will fail.

Let me remind you that it's okay. You will win some battles and you will lose others. The stretches between those wins will seem long sometimes. You will get discouraged. You will question what in the hell you've gotten yourself into. You will wonder if it's worth it.

The answer is YES.

The beauty of this journey is that every day is another opportunity. If you didn't get it right today, you have a fresh shot at it tomorrow. You can try again. You can change routes. You can scrap the plan and create a new one if you need to. The key is to just keep showing up.

Courage doesn't always roar. Sometimes courage is the quiet voice at the end of the day saying, "I'll try again tomorrow. —Maryanne Radmacher

#GoForIt 🔲🔲

When you look back over your success journey, you want a little dust in the mix. Now, this may sound a little strange, but you want to fail. If you don't how will get back up? How will you inspire the next person with a road that was too easy? How will you really appreciate the win if you didn't have to work, push, or sacrifice for it? I know you want to earn it. And failure is worth the price.

If you fail, what is the worst thing that could happen? Write that down.

If you fly, what is the best thing that could happen? Write that down too.

Failure teaches you to be stronger, to be better. Failure shows you where you went wrong so you can avoid those mistakes the next time around. Don't allow a fear of failure to hold you back from staring your dreams in the face. Don't doubt whether or not you can get back up. You will.

You've come too far.

Keep going.

Failing is a part of success. You have to fall down to get back up. – Tinarsha Brown **#GoForIt** 🔲🔲

Chapter 5

TAKE THE LEAP

Trust Yourself to Fly.

Like many other times before, I was teetering on the edge of a cliff.

It was time to decide if I was going to take the leap. Should I jump and (hopefully) find my wings in flight? Or should I stay right here—safe— and keep peering over the top of that mountain, wondering, waiting, and wishing?

It was now or never. I had everything I needed. Money in the bank. Happy clients who thankfully sent new people my way. My husband had my back with all of the support a woman could ask for. Yes I had everything I needed

Except full-on faith.

Life Is A Leap Of Faith

Now faith is confidence in what we hope for and assurance about what we do not see. —Hebrews 11:1 **#GoForIt** 🔲🔳

Life will constantly call you to take a leap of faith. It's always scary and you'll never feel fully prepared. Fear will get in your ear, in your spirit, and do everything it can to dissuade and discourage you. One more class. A little more money, a better car, a new house. If fear has its way, there will always be something more, something else, blocking you from your blessings.

All you really need is enough faith to take that leap. One small leap leads to a larger one. There will be leaps to take in your career. Leaps to take in your business. Leaps to take in love. Each one of those leaps are necessary. You need them. The bigger, the better.

> **Fear will tell you there's something else you need before you can walk towards the dreams and the destiny that's calling you. Don't listen.**
>
> **#GoForIt** 🅵🅸

Grab your faith and go.

You can't step out there on that shaky, I-Don't-Know-If-This-Is Gonna-Work faith, either. No. That just won't do. We're going *big*.

What you are setting out to do will require big faith.

You need to grab your no nonsense, I'm-Gonna-Do-What-I-Gotta-Do faith.

Your Push-Past-The-Naysayers faith.

Your It-Doesn't-Make-Sense-To-Anybody-Else faith.

Your I-May-Not-Have-It-Now-But-It's-Coming-Soon faith.

You need your Never-Give-Up faith.

So don't just pack any faith. Pack your real faith. Pack your bold faith. Pack your unshakable faith.

The biggest leaps you'll take in life can be from a cliff, but they can also be from the bottom of an abyss. Life will knock us down and while we're there, contemplating what to do next, we see everything that brought us to that place with more clarity. Our strength and our faith are renewed and we make the decision to take that big leap. Leaps can be your only way out of your circumstances. Take it.

****

It took me some time to warm up to the idea of becoming an agent, but once I was in, I was in. I fell in love with negotiating deals, especially the hard ones. If something seemed impossible, I was driven to get it done. You could make the mistake of telling me no if you wanted to. That one word—or even the thought of it—was all I needed to push me. I pushed myself harder than anyone else I knew at the table. If a deal came my way, I was going to close it. Period.

Every transaction, every client, just made me want more and more. More than a transaction, I saw the bigger picture. These weren't just houses—these were lives, dreams, and a sense of stability that some people never thought possible. Homeownership once felt so far out my reach, but there was something in me that told me it would happen someday. It did. So there was this fire inside of me to make the same reality true for as many people as I could. I saw my dreams in each one of them.

So even when I wanted to give up, I couldn't.

I still don't.

Believe In The Power Of Things You Cannot See

The year I decided to pursue real estate full time, I decided to create a vision board. That board would be my compass, my guiding path, a tangible visualization of everything I wanted for myself, my family, and my life that year. I sat at the table, surrounded by glue and scissors and flipping through magazines. I picked up one of my favorites, Essence, searching for pictures that stood out to me. I tore out a few and continued looking through the pages for more.

Then something caught my eye.

There was an image of a lady standing on a cliff. There was this big, bountiful tree in front of her, with one apple. Standing on her toes, she stretched and reached for that one apple. Below the image was a headline I'll never forget.

Step out on faith.

That was me and that was it. That was the word I needed to hear.

Step out on faith, Tinarsha.

I realized in that moment it was time. I wouldn't know until I tried. I had nothing to lose.

I had to take the leap.

I wish I could say it was all easy. When I decided to open my own brokerage, I felt fully prepared going in. I knew the business like back of my hand. I had clients and agents ready to service them. There wasn't a problem I'd met that I could not solve.

Yet, I still had more than my fair share of I-have-bitten-off-more-than-I can-chew moments. As soon as I crossed one hurdle, another took its place. I needed to find the right space. I needed more agents. My clients demanded more attention than ever. And the naysayers...

If I had a hundred dollar bill for every time someone asked me, "Why…?"

"Why do you want to open your own office?"

"How do you expect do get business?"

"Are you going to do all of this yourself?"

The questions—the doubt—just kept coming. It was a constant stream of static that I just couldn't turn off. There were those nos again, showing up as distractions and attempts to derail me from what I knew to be my path. Little did they know, those attempts to plant seeds of doubt in my mind only made me want it more. Naysayers are the best motivators.

I sought advice from people who I could trust to tell me the truth and to steer me in the right direction. I found a business coach and an accountability partner. I asked. I didn't hesitate to stick my hand in the air when I didn't know the answer. I prayed. I honored God's answers with my faith. And even in my moments of uncertainty, doors opened. I found the right space. I found the right people and they found me. Every step of faith proved to be more steady than the last. But I had to be willing to make the move.

I had to take the leap.

When I did, I realized I could fly.

You may not always have it all in front of you. If you did, faith wouldn't be necessary. Leaps of faith require us to be bold, ask less, and move more. You may not have the answers now. You may not be able to see the full picture or the road that will ultimately lead you to your destiny. That is okay. In fact, that is part of what makes this journey special. Imagine the story you'll have to tell when it's all said and done. (I hope to read about it one day.)

Today, I want you to decide what you are going to fly for. What dream is waiting for you? What vision have you buried under fear or doubt? Where have you pushed pause in your life when you really needed to step on the gas? Find *that*. Go after *that*. Chase *that*.

Find the fight in you. Never let it go.

And remember, big leaps mean big rewards. Take those big, beautiful leaps.

Without thinking, make a list of the leaps you want to take. Don't think about how big they are. Don't think why you can't do it. None of that matters. You want it. You deserve it. It's already yours.

Dreams are necessary to life. – Anais Nin

#GoForIt 🔖📷

Leaps Need Angels

I met Steven Lloyd for the first time in April 2014. He was one of the managers of a franchise real estate office in a city nearby and from day one, I always felt he was someone I could trust and turn to in business. He would always tell me I could call him for help. From time to time, he would shoot me an encouraging email or send a note card in the mail. He was an angel on my shoulder.

In November 2014, I was really overwhelmed with the growing pains of my new brokerage. Things were hard to say the least. I felt in over my head but I knew I wasn't giving up. But this thing was proving to be so much harder than I thought. God knew I needed some reassurance. My angel, Steven, showed up in a contracts class we were both enrolled in one afternoon. When he asked how the business was going, my challenges rambled out of me before he could even complete his sentence. We were approaching the 4th quarter of the year and I'd expected to be so much further than I was. I felt vulnerable. I felt scared. He understood it all.

After listening patiently to my woes, Steven gave me exactly what I needed in that moment. He told me that while my excitement and desire to win was on target, I shouldn't be so hard on myself. He reminded me it would take at least two years to build a solid office, and he knew because he'd done it before. He understood my pain. I felt my worries diminish in the presence of someone who could relate to me, someone who had been where I was and could encourage me to not be so hard on myself and to hang in there. It felt amazing.

The following week, I met with Steven to review my strategic plans and make some very essential changes to the way I was approaching some areas in my business. He showed me how to build a team, how to train a team, and how to stay laser focused on our goals. I took his advice and ran with it, and we had an incredible 2015 as a result. In 2016, we're on course to break our own records. Steven and I make time to brainstorm at least two to three times a month. He is a difference-maker in my life and in my business.

You don't have to leap alone. When we are looking to make things happen in our lives and to make shifts, we can't always do it by ourselves. Look for people who can support you. Check your inner circle and your industry circle. If you are leaping into a new industry, look for the best and reach out to them. There are angels out there who are waiting and willing to help you, and sometimes, hold you.

Destiny flocks together. – T.D. Jakes

#GoForIt

Before You Take Your Leap

If you are contemplating a leap, I don't want you to wait too long. This book was created to give you a push and I know you feel the momentum starting to build. You feel that passion starting to rise up. Your dreams are becoming real and colorful again. It's time to go for it.

Here are some steps to take today:

Ask somebody. Never underestimate the power of talking to people. When starting a new venture, reach out to your rolodex and search your network for anyone who is successfully doing what you want to do. Ask them questions. Study their successes and their failures. You'd be surprised at how much people are willing to share if you just ask. And there is nothing wrong with admitting you don't know.

See it before you can touch it. Dreams become real when there is a dollar sign attached to them. Write yourself a check for a wild, hairy amount. Something that terrifies you. Sign it with your name and then tape it up on a wall or stick it in your wallet. Look at it every day. Claim it and watch how easy it becomes to stretch yourself to make it a reality.

Create a blueprint. Write down your goals. Studies show that people who write down their goals achieve them at a significantly higher rate than those who don't. Figure out what you want to do and list what it will take to get there. No one drives to a place they've never been without a map or GPS. Your life is no different.

Chapter 6
NOTHING TO LOSE

You've Got This.

Confession: When I decided to step out on faith and pursue real estate full-time, I was terrified.

Yes I loved my clients and helping them to find the perfect homes to raise their families and build lives in.

Yes I loved the excitement of closing deals and the money that came along with them.

And yes, I was living my dream.

But no, I didn't want to let go of the good, secure job, benefits, stock options, or my retirement plan that I envisioned I would always have to fall back on. So as I contemplated whether or not this was the time to step out on my own, the first question on my mind wasn't focused on what I had to gain. Instead I had to ask myself:

What did I have to lose?

Just everything I'd worked all of my adult life to get. And keep.

When you grow up without, not only do you work harder to get it, you work even harder to keep it. I knew what it was like to be homeless, to be hungry, to not know what you would have or where you would be from one day to the next. So security was very important to me and my full-time job gave me that. My paycheck provided the certainty of a salary and an assurance that I could pay my bills. I had my husband, but we were a two-income household. Like most families, we were looking to bring more money into our house, not less.

In real estate, if you don't work, you don't get paid. It's all on you—finding clients, closing deals, and making it happen. No excuses allowed. Not to mention I'd had my share of sweet deals and some...not so much. There were times when I would work for weeks to get a deal closed, on the phone practically day and night, running from one office to next, only to make $1.55 an hour once the transaction was all said and done. Yet I loved every minute of it and with my job, I could afford to have a few of those less-than ideal deals and still be okay. It was all about the passion because I didn't have to worry about a paycheck.

But leaving my job would change all of that.

I was at the crossroad every entrepreneur faces at some point or another. Take the risk, follow my passion, and go for it—or stay put and play it safe.

Passion is a word that feels really big, doesn't it? We all have it, but sometimes we have to dig deep to find it. Our passion can be muted by life, responsibilities, lack of financial resources or support from the people we love, but it's actually our compass—a guiding force leading us to what's next. Whenever you are at a point of decision about whether to take one turn or the next, check your passion compass.

What is it telling you to do?

Follow, follow, follow...

My passion for real estate grew from a seed planted in me as a little girl. As a kid, I promised myself I would own my own home. We were evicted so much and I decided early that one day, I would have my own. No notices on the door. No one telling me I had to get out. No embarrassment or shame from seeing my things on the street. I would be in charge. Assisting my mother in her real estate business watered the seed and it only grew when I purchased my first home with my husband. There was something inside of me telling me to go for it. It wasn't about the money. It was about my passion. It was about following something I loved and trusting it would sustain me.

Following your passion and deciding to go for your dreams is a decision.

#GoForIt

I knew, in the end, along with my faith, I'd have my passion to fall back on.

Once you've prayed, researched, planned, discussed, and thought it out, there is only thing left to do. Decide.

The Real Question...

What do you really have to lose?

Often, what we perceive to be holding us back from what we really want is more comfort than necessity. For some of us, that's a cushy job and a great salary. I am not saying we don't all need income and stability, but can that business you've always wanted to start provide that? What can you sacrifice today to live your dreams tomorrow?

Don't allow a dependency on the paycheck to keep you from your purpose. If you have a dream to start your own business, map out the plan. You have to determine what you want more—clenching what you have and staying planted or releasing the present for your purpose.

There is a popular picture you have probably seen circulating on social media. In it, God is knelt down in front of a little girl, with one hand outstretched towards her. His other hand is hidden behind His back and in it is a huge teddy bear. The little girl is hugging a significantly smaller bear to her chest and you can tell she adores it. The caption above her head reads something like, "But I love this one."

Sound familiar?

This picture is exactly how we stand firm in our lives. There is something amazing waiting for us on the other side, but we refuse to let go and to leap out on faith. We focus so much on what there is to lose, but we lose sight of all the possibilities that come with following your destined path to determine where it leads.

I'll ask you this— what will you gain if you decide to go for your dream?

When it gets hard (and it most certainly will), you will have to find your faith, focus on the gain, and most importantly, stay the course. And brace yourself for the challenges, the bumps in the road, that are sure to come and shake you. It's all just a test to see how bad you really want it. I promised you truth from the beginning, so...

Once you make the decision to go for it and trust your faith, the real struggle begins. Everything that can go wrong? Probably will.

Releasing my big teddy bear/security blanket/salary was just the first step for me. And honestly, I wasn't prepared—mentally or financially—for everything headed my way that first year when I opened my brokerage in 2013. My leap of faith from part-time to a full-time agent in 2005 was graceful and I did so well. I expected the next leap a few years later, which was going out fully on my own, to be similar. I wasn't naïve enough to think there wouldn't be any challenges, but the road was much bumpier than I thought.

My business was young and my team was essentially non-existent. So that meant I had to wear all of the hats—including agent. I was the broker, the accountant, human resources, and the marketing department, on a slow day. There were so many moving pieces to running an office and finding clients and sales that my head stayed in a constant state of spin, frustration, and worry. From the moment I opened the doors, it felt as if the levees broke. My savings account dwindled as my fear rose. We weren't closing enough deals and I was pouring way more money into the business than I was drawing out. Cue the chorus of fear.

About nine months into 2014, the once-determined song in my head that replayed, "Go for it! Get it! You got this!" over and over, had become, "What did you get yourself into?" That soundtrack of doubt played so loudly until I started to panic.

Fear threatened to hold me down—to make me quit—but I hadn't come this far to fail. Turning back wasn't an option. Giving up was out of the question. No U-turns allowed. No I wasn't going to turn around. I decided I just needed to change course. I figured if I could just get some steady cash flow coming in, I could continue to build the brokerage without so much pressure to keep our lights on. I had to do something—fast. Panicked and in full-on survival mode, I packed my humility and did the only thing that made sense to me in the moment.

I looked for a job.

My undercover job search (I was too embarrassed to tell anyone I was looking) led me to a timeshare sales position nearby. I knew I could excel at property sales with my eyes closed and since the office was only open from 6:00am to 1:00 pm every day, I figured I could still run my office in the late afternoons when we were busiest. I interviewed with the sales manager and the director and waited on pins and needles for a week until the company called me back with an offer. I never thought I'd be relieved to hear the words, "You're Hired" again in my life, but I was. This was the relief I'd been hoping for and I was all set to start until the company asked me to surrender my real estate license. As a condition of employment, I couldn't sell real estate in any capacity while working for them.

I resigned before I even started.

Back to square one, I needed a fast Plan B. My two must-haves were flexibility and steady cash, with an emphasis on the flexibility, so I knew a traditional desk gig wouldn't work. A friend suggested I consider Uber and, in the moment, it sounded ideal. I was used to driving clients all over the city anyway and I could even show properties in between rides. Without sharing with mentors, accountability partners, or even my husband, I signed on one day and within a few days, I was on the road as a part-time Uber driver with a huge U plastered on my windshield. For months, I tried to maintain a crazy schedule of working at the office all day and Ubering at night, napping in the car for a few hours in between. The exhaustion, the tears, and the struggle were so real. Yet my desire and determination to do this outweighed my fears. Even on those days when I didn't think the possible was possible, I kept pushing.

I realized that I actually did have something to lose. It wasn't the appreciation and applause from people I knew. It wasn't even my pride or the money. It was the promise I made to myself that *I would never give up*.

I had to keep going—for me. And that meant sacrificing my Uber coins to get back to giving the business my all. I tucked my U decal into my glove compartment (I still keep it in there as a reminder) and refocused all of my energy into the office.

A few weeks later, I sat on the phone with one of my mentors who ran a multi-million dollar real estate company. In the presence of someone who I knew could really understand the space I was in, I poured my heart out to him. I got real raw, real honest, real quick. This first year just wasn't what I envisioned. This was far from easy. In fact, it was ten thousand times harder.

"Tinarsha, if it were easy everyone would be doing it." Simple truth. I was so used to winning in life, always making it happen for myself even when it was hard, that I'd lost sight of the truth. Nothing worth having was easy. And this business was no exception. No this wouldn't be easy. But it damn sure wasn't impossible.

My lightbulb was already on and that conversation just amplified the wattage. I regrouped and followed two key pieces of advice my mentor offered—focus on building my team and training them to be successful. Focus. That's what it all boiled down to. Failing permanently had never been an option—not now, not ever.

Some say a star shines the brightest when the night is darkest. Dreams may feel like clouds, but there are those real moments—up close—when they go dark. The money runs out. The plans fail. The people and their promises scatter. You have no idea what to do next. Here's a hint...

Look up.

If you quit—quitting will become easier and easier for the rest of your life. – *Osman Minkara* **#GoForIt** 🔲🔳

Whatever You Do, Don't Quit

When you feel like quitting (and you will), here is the most sound, most impactful, most sincere bit of advice I can give you. *Don't.*

Quitting on your dreams in motion is quitting on your purpose. And your purpose is not one of those things that allow you to check in and check out.

What you get is yours to keep. It was assigned to you to carry out.

There is no stop. There is just delay. So stopping isn't giving you a way out.

It is only hitting your reset button.

Tough times can wash away every memory of every stride you've ever made. In an instant, you are questioning everything—your decisions, your judgement, and your common sense. Nothing feels as if it's going right or will go right again. What was once a little hard feels like it might break you. What was once possible feels like no way in hell. Once your mind starts moving in the wrong direction, it becomes a snowball effect. Now what?

Go back to where you started. Do you remember your Day One? Do you remember that moment when you had no idea how you would make it work? But you did. And then another moment of despair came and you made it through. And then another. Before you knew it, you were where you are now.

You did it once and you'll do it again.

Don't look to the left or to the right anymore—comparing yourself to someone who has no purpose on your path. Keep pushing. Keep praying. Keep believing that you've got this. (Because you do.)

And, whatever you do, don't give up now.

ONE MORE THING...

I am a big believer in goals. As I mentioned before, I am not a small-goal type. I believe your goals should be big. They should scare you. If they don't, reevaluate them. Step it up a notch (or twenty). Instead of imagining yourself at the beginning or at the start of your path, picture yourself at the end—winning. What does that look like? How do you feel?

While you are on your way...

1. Keep the vision in front of you: Creating a vision board was a pivotal moment for me. My dreams became tangible and more real to me as I began to see them take shape in front of me. Put your dreams on paper, be it on a vision board or writing them down and hanging them all over your office or your home. *See* them every day and all day if you have to. The point is to not allow your mind to lose sight of where you are headed.

2. Be extravagant in your choices and your dreams: Don't play small! If you don't dream big for yourself, no one else will. You only get what you ask for so why not ask for all of it?

3. Don't settle: Taking small steps towards your goals is not the same as settling. Don't accept anything less than what you want or you deserve. You determine your worth. Once you set your value for your time, your expertise, and your skills, stay committed to that. Increase, never decrease.

Getting Clear

Ask yourself these questions as you begin to form your next-step plan:

- Do I Care Too Much About What People Think?
- Who Am I Sharing My Big Dreams With?
- Do I Say Yes Enough?
- What Bold Step Can I Take Today Towards My Big Goal?
- Am I Playing Full Out In My Life? If Not, What Is Holding Me Back?
- What Am I Afraid Of?
- Do I Give Myself Permission To Fail Enough?
- What Do I Want To Be Remembered For?

"Don't let your fear hold your passion hostage, you have nothing to lose once you release the fear" - *Tinarsha Brown*

#GoForIt ◼◻

Chapter 7
LET GO OF YESTERDAY

There is always something greater.

And no one puts new wine into old wineskins. For the wine would burst the wineskins, and the wine and the skins would both be lost. New wine calls for new wineskins. – Mark 2:22 **#GoForIt** 🔲🔲

I knew my marriage was over long before it actually was.

Once inseparable and as close as a man and woman could be, an emotional distance grew between us that I couldn't explain. They say the eyes are the window to the soul, and in his, I saw what his mouth wanted to tell me, but held back. The same eyes that looked at me as if I was the only woman on earth. The eyes that filled with tears as I walked down the aisle to become his wife. The eyes that watched our children with so much pride at their games and school awards ceremonies. Those eyes—were now cold.

As women, we all have that intuition—when God speaks to our spirit—that tells us when it's time. I was no different. I felt something. Like so many other women, I turned my head. Yes, I knew there was something going on. But this was my husband, my family—my life. So as much as I wanted to know, I didn't, at least not then. It was easier to be safe, to live in the hope of what could be instead of the reality of what was.

I knew it was over. I just needed God to confirm what I already knew.

****

My husband and I had been married for twenty years and had loved each other for twenty-four. When I met him, I was on the cusp on becoming a full-fledged woman—in that precious space in time in your twenties right between girlhood and womanhood when you are not quite who you will be, but you have a strong enough handle on who you are. Our hearts were young and open, and so our love was strong, pure, and true.

He was a part of me, my soulmate, my partner, in every sense of the word.

Together, we built a life that movie scenes and little girl dreams were made of. A big, five-bedroom, five-bath home in the suburbs. Three children who were all beautiful, smart, and talented. I could not have asked God for anything more or written this story more perfectly. This man was my king and I was his queen.

Until one day I wasn't.

At the beginning of 2015, two days before my birthday, I found out that my husband had a two-year-old son. And he wasn't mine.

Two weeks prior, I began to pray to God for an answer. There was something strong gripping my spirit and I couldn't shake it or press the ignore button anymore. "God, I need to close out what shouldn't be or close out a chapter of my life I shouldn't be in. But I need to make sense of what is going on." I gave those words to God over and over, believing Him for my answers. I was caught between a place of peace and uncertainty, but I knew change had become necessary.

I just needed it to make sense. I needed to hear Him. I needed assurance.

Soon, I'd have the assurance and the answer I'd prayed for. And it devastated me. My mind knew the reality, but my heart and my body refused to accept what I knew to be true. I spent a lot of time tossing and turning, grieving, replaying scenarios in my head. I would spend hours every day tormenting my soul and my spirit with thoughts and questions, trying to retrace the moment when things went so wrong.

Could I forgive him?

Could I move past this?

Despite the devastation and humiliation I felt, there was a part of me that wanted to fix it. My children were hurt and angry. Our home was falling apart at the seams. I was losing my man, my marriage—everything that I thought would be forever. But I still loved him.

I had to let go.

A month later, I went into the hospital for a routine procedure on my breast. My doctor felt things went well and we both expected the results to come back normal. At my follow-up appointment a week or so later, she found a hematoma and necrosis, both of which prevented oxygen from circulating to my breast. I'd developed blood clots and was rushed in for an emergency surgery. The reality hit me that I didn't have my husband by my side. He was still physically living in our home, but my husband was gone.

And soon, my breast would be too.

But not my strength. Or my life.

While I recovered from my surgery, God granted me a strength I didn't believe I had. I knew it was time and I was ready. I started clearing it out my life. I knew if I was going to truly start over, I had to have a clean slate. A fresh start. *New wine skins.*

God met me where I was.

And I stood right up to grab everything He had for me.

Finally, I let go.

There are good things waiting to manifest for you. But you have to be willing to let go. – Sheila Green **#GoForIt** 🖊️🔲

When It's Time, It's Time

Growth happens in spurts. We see it in our children. We see it in our gardens as seasonal changes slowly coax flowers and trees into full bloom. When things start to grow, they take on a new shape and a new form.

Growth is a sense of awareness that what was once new is now old.

Growth is about leaving things behind.

Growth also comes with signs. Depending on how open and receptive we are to the idea, it can bring anxiety or agitation. We may feel overwhelmed and weighed down. We may fall out of love with a person, our careers, or our lives as a whole. The very things we once loved more than anything else just don't thrill us anymore.

That's a sign that it's time to leave those things behind. A new season has arrived.

When your passion weans, you do more harm than good when you linger too long. Out of a sense of obligation or a fear of releasing the familiar, we want to cling to what we have. If the thrill is gone, too often we stay. But we aren't showing up fully or giving our all.

We're not committed to being the best or seeking results. And that is not only unfair to the person or the situation—it's unfair to us.

What are you holding on to that no longer belongs in your life? List them. Bless them. Let them go.

> There is a new season waiting for you once you've made the room to receive it. Look around you and decide what needs to go. It's time for you to grow.
>
> #GoForIt 🅵🅸

It was a layoff that enabled me to grow into full-time entrepreneurship in real estate. It was the end of a marriage that allowed me to grow into a full love. I grew alongside my calling. If it's time to move on, it's time.

What Is Not For You May Be For Someone Else

When it is time for us to release something, it is not always about us. Holding on—outstaying our season—could be hindering someone else from moving into their position. We move on to our next space or assignment to allow them to step into the void and fill it. It is now theirs.

And it's no longer ours.

The home I shared with my husband was our dream house. I'd worked so hard to make that home possible for us. We'd raised our children there. We'd celebrated anniversaries and holidays there. And even though our marriage had ended, I wanted to hold on to our house. For me it represented more than where we lived— it was a piece of us. I just wasn't ready to let it go. After I divorced, I moved into a new beautiful home where my children and I could start over and rebuild, but I kept the keys to my old home close with no intention of letting go. At least not anytime soon.

One afternoon, I received a call from a former client. I'd helped her with a home purchase and shortly after that, her husband died. She was too emotionally tied to the home they shared and she wanted to sell it, so she called me for help. We found her a new house, but a year later she called wanting to move again. She didn't feel comfortable or settled in the new space. For her, it still wasn't home. Figuring she was still on an emotional rollercoaster from her loss, I suggested she wait for a while to see if she would change her mind. She agreed.

Six months later, she came back to me. She was still adamant about moving, and despite my efforts to try to convince her otherwise, she wanted a new home.

I invited her to lunch and we began to talk through exactly what she wanted in a house. She was very specific about everything—even down to the size of the yard. Her husband had built an elaborate playset for her children and she wanted to make sure it would fit. As she continued to describe her dream home, I began to envision it too. Everything she wanted, I already had.

It was the home I had been holding on to.

I asked her to hop in her car and follow me. I drove her to the house and from the moment she stepped out of the car, she was in love. After a quick walk through, she asked if she could leave to pick up her children to see the place. When they all returned, the kids walked from room to room claiming their spaces. We both had daughters and her little girl loved the fact that there was a bathroom in the room that would be hers. My daughter had enjoyed that too.

God brought this woman and her children to me for a reason. This family was finally home.

And I could finally let go.

This was the last step I needed to take to close out that season of my life. In this process, I rebuilt my courage. I keep moving—never looking back. I knew I had to let go of everything I wasn't connected to anymore. Everything. Including the guilt, shame, and fear.

I had emptied everything, including my bank account, to prepare for the new things to come. I sold my wedding ring. I put ads for all of my furniture on Craigslist. I started my life over from scratch—new home, new furniture, and a new state of mind. And the new, better things came in abundance. I received my insurance license, became a mortgage broker, and made more money in real estate than I ever had in my career. I had a beautiful new home and a beautiful new love. When I was willing to clear the clutter from my life and from my spirit, the floodgates of more opened up. My soul and my spirit opened up.

And so did everything else around me.

Clear the clutter—physical and mental—from your life. If it reminds you of a season of your life that has passed, remove it. It doesn't matter how valuable it looks now. Your purpose can not thrive in a crowded space. If it doesn't feed your purpose, it has to go.

There is better waiting.

But you have to make room first—for you and for the person who is waiting to receive what is no longer yours.

Fear and familiarity will keep you stuck. – *Sheila Green*

#GoForIt 📘 📷

Why Don't We Let Go?

Women, by nature, are fiercely loyal. We fight for what's ours—even when it no longer serves us. People, friends, jobs, clients, habits, financial situations. Even dreams we once had.

We hang in there. But there is such a thing as being loyal to a fault. We allow fear and familiarity to keep us stuck in seasons that are no longer for us. A 2014 study from the American Sociological Association found that women are four times more likely to stay at job with diminished potential than men, and those numbers only increase for mothers.

We have to learn to let go.

How do you let go?

1. **Take control of your life and decide what makes you happy.** Don't hold on to things to make others happy. This is your life and you only get one to live. Be true to yourself about what is no longer good for you and love yourself more than you love others' opinions. Turn the noise off and live your life.

2. **Put your mask on first.** If you've ever been on an airplane, what is one of the first things the flight attendant tells you as she reads the safety instructions? "Put your mask on first, and then reach over the help the person next to you." We're giving everyone else oxygen and holding our breath to make sure they are breathing while we're suffering. Breathe for you first, and then help everyone else around you.

3. **Make room.** You can't have it all. You don't have room for the bad and the better, so choose.

4. **Pray.** God will give you the strength you need. Ask Him.

5. **Be Positive.** Start tomorrow expecting it will be your best. **If you believe it, it's yours.**

Take Control

As women, we shy away from the idea that we should have control over the outcomes in our lives. Society tells us who we should be. Social media tells us what we should look like. The companies we work for tell us how we should lead, if we're given the opportunity to lead at all. For most of us, so many of our decisions are made for us—led by our circumstances rather than our choices.

I want you to start thinking and acting differently. I want you deciding more, standing up more, and speaking more.

I want you to take control of your life.

Taking control begins with your mind. Set your mind on the outcome you want to create for yourself. Decide where you want to go and how you want to get there. Stand firm in that. Don't allow anyone else's agenda or opinions to sway or deter you. *Stand firm.*

You have to decide that regardless of what you're going through, how hurt you are, or how much you want to change the people or person who may be responsible for your pain that you are not a victim.

Yes—some things happened to you.

Yes— some people hurt you.

Yes— life, right now, may not be exactly how you planned.

But tomorrow is a new day. You can change your circumstances. You can be happy. Your children can be happy. You can make the money you want and need to make. You can have the career you desire.

You can take control of your life.

Make the choice. And everything else will fall into place.

You will never get what you deserve if you won't let go of what you already have.
— Sheila Green **#GoForIt**

Chapter 8
UNDER RECONSTRUCTION

You can begin again... and again.

I am going to make tomorrow a good day. For me. – Sheila Green
#GoForIt 🔵🔵

In business and in life, rebuilding is not only inevitable, it's necessary. It is a painful, yet beautiful, process. It hurts. It tests. It teaches.

And our rebuilding always begins with a storm.

Have you ever been outside or watching from the window right before a storm starts? The air changes. What starts as a warm, light breeze transitions to a heavy, fast-paced wind. Trees start bending, leaves are whipping around, and anything that is not nailed down starts whirling around too. Stuff may get torn up or torn down from the force. Clouds become thick, the sky darkens. You know the rain is coming—lots of it. Before you know it, it's here. Fast and furious. Depending on where you are, a storm's duration can feel like a lifetime. Minutes can feel like hours, hours like days. But regardless of how long a storm lasts, what do we know is coming at some point?

The sun.

The sun reminds us that the clouds, thunder, and rain were only temporary. The sun means things are alright again. The sun is a sign that it's safe to come outside and piece together what's been torn apart. The sun is the reemergence of life light—the fulfilled promise of greatness—that awaits us on the other side.

The sun is the lesson.

Every storm you'll endure in this life will come with its own lessons. You likely won't recognize them in the midst of all of that wind and pouring rain, but they're there. And they never leave you. Those lessons become the core of who you are—your DNA—and will fuel you forward for the next assignment and the next level you are being called to ascend to. You'll come back to them again and again, along with the reminder of how hard-won your lessons, your sun, really was.

A storm looks like loss, but it is actually renewed life.

A storm looks like an insurmountable challenge, but it is actually a second (or maybe fourth) chance to get it right.

A storm looks like pain, but it is really purpose.

A storm looks like disaster, but it is actually your destiny.

Bottom line: *You have to go through it to get to it.*

It's all about a decision to pick up your pieces and rebuild again.

Rebuilding, in any aspect of our lives, is about growth—it stretches us, demanding a shift towards something new, something more, something greater. When we're temporarily (emphasis on temporary) torn down, we always come back stronger than ever.

Notice I didn't say we would come back the same.

Think about the World Trade Center after the September 11th terrorist attacks. Two of the tallest, strongest structures in the world, they represented power inside and out. When those buildings fell—one by one—a part of our country, of our spirit, was lost forever. It felt like the end. We didn't know if New York City, or America, would ever be the same.

Then something incredible happened.

Firefighters risked their lives to save people trapped inside an inferno of smoke and flames.

People poured into the streets to help each other. Compassion flooded into the city from all around the world. Regardless of what we looked like, where we lived, or where we were born, our pain united us. We were all Americans in that moment.

In 2002, reconstruction at the World Trade Center site began. In 2006, the doors to a new building opened. And soon, another. And eventually there will be others. Even if the physical nature of those buildings has changed, the energy surrounding it is different. More significant. Stronger.

Will the World Trade Center be exactly the same? No, it won't be. But those buildings will be strong. They will be cherished. They will be an ever-present symbol of greatness and what America endured.

They will be back.

So while we may lose some things, we always come away stronger, more solid, and more sound than we ever thought possible.

Don't be so afraid to lose that you miss an opportunity to gain.

The demand to rebuild comes out of nowhere. When we least expect it. We're rolling along with life, doing everything we're supposed to do. We are going to a job every day or helping our clients in our businesses. We are raising our children and being the best wives we know how to be.

We think our lives are moving in the right direction. We feel we're doing our best and giving it our all. We're praying hard enough, showing up and working enough. Yet a storm comes, knocks us off our feet, and tears some stuff up in our lives. *But I was doing everything I was supposed to do! Why is this happening to me?* We've all be there, right?

It is not always about what you did wrong—instead it's about what has to be made right. It is not always about what you aren't doing—sometimes it is about what you need to do next. Rebuilding is not about focusing on what you already have. It is about getting what you need.

If you are going to chase your destiny, you will need some things you don't have right now. It may be a new set of skills, new people and relationships, or maybe even new money.

One thing's for sure—you will need a strength you didn't know you had.

In March 2015, I arrived at my doctor's downtown office. It was morning, and I walked in slowly—my pain forcing my body to slow down to a pace that felt more like a crawl than a walk. I moved deeper into the office, closer to her. Our eyes locked, and I noticed that hers had filled with tears. She fought hard to hold them back, but within minutes, the weight of the water won, and her cheeks were wet.

She said the words no woman ever wants to hear.

"We had to remove your left breast."

Dealing with divorce and recovering from my surgery, I was already in the wind. Now it was time for the rain.

My breast. Gone. Reconstructive surgery and a prosthetic. Necessary. Time stood still. I couldn't move. My soul wasn't prepared for this. Still teetering on an emotional edge from losing my marriage and this unexpected battle with my health in what felt like the same breath, I couldn't find any more tears as my doctor cried next to me. She knew, like I knew, that a woman's breast is a part of her essence, defining her femininity and her beauty for herself and the world. *Who would I be without a piece of my body? Would I look the same? Would I feel the same? Would I be the same?*

I was hurting—physically and emotionally. I was depressed. I was alone. My body was bruised and weak. My breast was gone. My heart was broken into a million tiny pieces. I was the lowest I'd ever been.

I was in a storm.

I didn't know the lesson God wanted me to gain from everything that was happening to me in that moment. But I knew it wasn't by circumstance that all of this happened at the same time. Losing my breast was so symbolic of what was going on around me and in my life. The things that were most precious to me—my husband, our home, my family, and my body as I'd always known it—were disappearing. If I can be honest with you, I didn't think I would ever come back from this. The sun was hidden so far behind the darkness that I didn't know if I would see it again.

At heart, I've always been a fighter. Faced with this storm, this fight, I knew I had to come through it. I'd have to fight through the pain, the hurt, and the loss. Step by step, piece by piece, I had to rebuild my life. The prosthetic and physical healing brought my body back. Prayer and patience brought my mind back.

A decision to win brought my spirit back.

2015 was still going to be my best year ever.

I decided I would make more money than I'd ever made.

I decided I would take better care of my body and love my physical self more.

I decided my family would be stronger.

And I did every single one of those things and more.

The year started out as my worst. But it ended it becoming my best.

Ride out your storms. Reconstruct your life.
#GoForIt

Rock bottom became the solid foundation on which I rebuilt my life. – J.K. Rowling **#GoForIt**

Strength Comes With The Storm

Before we can reconstruct, we mourn what we've lost. We grieve what was, what could be, and what should have been. It is often in the reconstructing process that our most significant *a ha* moments happen—when it clicks that there is a lesson to be learned. We realize we didn't just lose something, but we *gained* something far greater. Strength. Clarity. A deeper, more profound sense of meaning and appreciation for what is left.

We lose someone we love and the family members we have left instantly become more precious. We lose our jobs or our homes and when we find new ones, the overtime, the long, car-packed

Constance Carter, Tinarsha Brown and Sheila Green

commute, or the mortgage payment don't feel as burdensome as it did before. We lose love and our next time around is so much sweeter.

Here's what I want you to get—don't be afraid to rebuild. When something falls apart in your life, look for the silver lining. Look for the lesson God wants to leave on your soul and spirit. Look for the strength you discovered to turn your life, your family, or your business around.

Your triumph is often wrapped in your tragedy.

When life throws you a punch, you don't have the option to stay down. If you give in, if you refuse to fight, what will you sacrifice? What will you lose? What's the cost for you and people who need you to show up for?

Are you willing to let your dreams die because you threw up your hands and gave up?

You will lose big contracts. You will lose a job. You may lose a home or husband. And the wind—your very next breath—will be knocked out of you. (I'll be the first to tell you it will hurt like hell.) But you don't get to lay down. You don't get to quit. This is your peace and happiness at stake. Your dreams are on the line. Everything you've claimed, everything you've worked for, every bit of greatness—every ray of sun—that has been promised to you.

This is your life.

You have one choice.

Get up. Put on your gloves.

And fight for it.

If you just keep breathing, you cannot be conquered. – Oprah Winfrey

#GoForIt 🔵🔵

Don't Keep Your Dreams Waiting

In 2009, my mother called me. "I had a dream about you," she started. She was extremely intuitive and I'd learned over the years to listen when she had a message for me. Chances were some variation of what she would share with me would manifest in my life. I settled in to listen.

She went on to tell me that she'd seen me in her sleep two nights in a row. In her dreams, I was in a struggle—a huge battle. This conflict was not physical, but I was going up against somebody big at the company I currently worked for as an IT Manager. After recounting the details of her dream, my mother assured me everything would work out in my favor. "You will be victorious. You will win."

Soon after my conversation with my mom, I received a call from a girlfriend. She, too, had dreamt about me recently and was anxious to share. Similar to my mother's dream, she told me a big challenge was coming my way and I was being prepared to make a move. "People will rally around you. There will be a circle of people around you. They will be cheering for you."

I had no idea what any of this meant, but I would soon find out.

A few weeks later, a manager called me into the office. He went on to tell me that there had been some "red flags" raised about how I was managing my department at the time and it had been decided that the management hierarchy in our division needed to change. As a result of the shift, I would now be reporting to someone who was, just a few a minutes ago, my peer and who happened to be a white man. I knew this person wasn't more qualified than me. I was shocked at what I heard. I'd been an exceptional employee and manager. Yet, in months prior, I began to like my job less and less. The salary was great though, so I convinced myself that I needed to suck it up and settle. I wondered if this situation meant something more. *Was God trying to get my attention?*

In that moment, the dreams my mother and friend had shared with me came back to my mind. This must have been the battle they were talking about. I was a target now. And I felt resistance building up against me. But I also felt something more, something bigger, at stake. This wasn't just about me.

The company I worked for had a history of discriminatory behavior. There was a small, but growing, group of minority employees, including single mothers and senior employees, who'd been wrongfully terminated or disciplined in some way. I'd heard their stories. And now I had a first-hand experience of my own. I'd been listening to their accounts and had been willing to be a shoulder of support, but I was never vocal to anyone about what I'd heard or seen. These were minorities just like me. They'd been targeted just like me. And now I had to do something about it.

I began working alongside the wronged employees to file formal complaints. I found attorneys. I accompanied them to the appropriate federal agencies to file their grievances. I challenged the CIO on their behalf. I became their advocate. I became their voice.

In the midst of it all, God revealed to me that there was something bigger for me once I completed this task. He delivered on that promise. I accepted a new position with a new company. I began to feel stronger and became more vocal in a marriage that sometimes rendered me silent about what I really needed and wanted. I was clearer. I was bolder. I was emerging as a new version of me that would only continue to show up more fully in my life and my work. And the employees I fought for were all vindicated.

If I had hesitated to step up into what I was being called to do, I would not have gained the wisdom, the strength, and the voice to shift other areas of my life. That experience was a stepping stone for me along the journey I am on now.

Had I allowed fear to set in, the dreams I am living out today may still be waiting.

If you are being spurred to move into action, move now. There is something significant at stake that you may not be able to see, but trust the process. Trust the first step you should take and allow the rest to unfold.

It may be your first step to rebuilding your life and starting anew.

Chapter 9
IT'S HOW YOU FINISH, NOT HOW YOU START

Run Your Race.

I was a runner for most of my high school years. I played other sports, but I loved track. It appears almost effortless, but it's really one of those this-isn't-as-easy-as-it-looks type of sports.

A lot like success.

Just like any sport, track is just as much about mind as it is body. It's a sport of strength, distance, and endurance. It's about pushing harder and going faster, even when you don't think you can. It's about jumping higher. Most of all, track is about finishing. Strong.

In my senior year, my relay team was one of the best in the region. As we neared the end of the season, we'd made it all the way to sectionals—the final meet before the state finals. The top three fastest times and performances from each event would advance to the state championships. Our team was strong, both individually and as a collective. Three members of our 4 x 100 team were also part of the 4 x 400 team. We'd all worked so hard to get here and this final race, the 4 x 400 relay, was the only thing between us and a chance to compete at the California State Championship Meet. We were ready for this. I felt it and I know everyone else did too. We had this.

I felt really strong, well, except for one thing. I'd pulled my hamstring earlier in the season and while it had healed enough for me to run without any real issues, subconsciously I still felt a little unsure. But my team and I needed this, so I had to push past my own insecurities and show up.

I kneel down, bow my head, and wait for the sound of the starting gun to hit the air. *Pop!* I take off, baton in hand. I start off strong, but within minutes, something shifts. As I am running, my mind becomes less and less clear and more and more cluttered. My hamstring feels fine, actually it feels better than it has in weeks, but my thoughts began to overtake my strength. *I hope my leg doesn't mess up. Did you feel that? Was that my hamstring about to pull? Am I gonna make it?* The discouraging, false thoughts just kept coming and my body began to respond. What started as a quiet whisper soon grew into a booming voice of fear. I felt my confidence slipping away and instead of pushing harder, I pulled back. I was at the point in the race when usually my adrenaline would fire up and I'd kick it in, pushing past the other runners to pass the baton to the second leg—the other girl waiting to run the next lap. My signature move was to sprint it in and leave the field, a trail of uniforms behind me in a blur. But today I was off.

My self-doubt didn't just slow me down, it crushed my team. It was a trickle effect. When I handed the baton off to the second leg, I noticed she wasn't giving it her all. And when she handed off to the third leg, she definitely didn't run her fastest. By the time the baton reached the anchor, the final sprinter, we didn't have a chance. I didn't just pass a baton. I'd passed my fear right along with it.

Had I focused on running my race instead of my injury, we could have won. Even though my thoughts started to move in the wrong direction, I could have reeled them back in, finished the race strong, and shown up for my team when they needed me most. But my thoughts played an evil trick on me. And I fell for it.

In my mind, my leg wasn't strong enough to support me.

In my mind, I needed to slow down to prevent myself from getting hurt again.

In my mind, I'd already lost the race.

I was so disappointed in myself, but my loss was nothing in comparison to my teammate. This meet was our anchor's only shot at the finals. She wasn't on the 4 x 100 team and she was relying on us collectively to guarantee her trip to the state championships. And because of me, she wouldn't be there. The look in her eyes haunted me for years after that and I will never forget it. I had a chance to pick up my pace—to help my team to win—and I didn't. My faith faltered. I lost confidence in myself.

I lost focus on the finish line.

That experience taught me two invaluable lessons. For the first time, I really got what it meant to be a part of a team. I'd been an athlete practically all of my life, but for some reason, there was a part of me that still saw myself as one person in the midst of the group as opposed to a part of it. I had my responsibility and they had theirs—I didn't get the dependency and reliance we all had on each other. But in that moment on the field, seeing the disappointment in my teammate's eyes, I realized I had a responsibility to her and everyone else on my team. I owed it to them to be my best and to give my all. From that day forward, I vowed to never let down my team again. I've had times in my life when that option would have been so much easier and not showing up would have been warranted. But when there is someone else looking to me to show up for them, I don't have a choice. And neither do you.

When you give up, who else are you holding back? So often, we think about dreams and the big things we want in life in the context of just us. If we don't pursue our goals, or if we go after them and fail, we take that disappointment on as if it's ours to own alone. And over time, it may be easier to deal with and sweep under the rug because there is no one else to be accountable to. But what about your team—be it a family, a community, or even those people who you haven't even met yet that will be your future employees or partners. What about them? Their destiny could be riding on you, waiting on you to show up. Don't let them down.

Something else I learned was that things can get off to a bad start, but that doesn't always mean a bad ending. As I ran my race, there was a moment when I could have shifted. Once I realized I had the strength to push, I could have, but I didn't. Fear kept me bound. If I had granted myself permission to finish the race differently, that story would have a much different ending.

Fight past your willingness to throw your hands up when you don't start strong. Setbacks don't mean stop—they mean pause, change course, and keep going.

#GoForIt 🅕 🅖

You have to resist the temptation to abandon your already-in-progress dreams for something new because it got hard. You could give up right before the best part comes—before you taste the sweetness of success. Before you finish your race.

Have you ever watched a baby learning to walk? She may go from crawling, to pulling up on something higher to get to her feet, and eventually, she can stand on her own. Soon, she gets the courage to take a step. She's wobbly, uncertain, but she keeps going. The first few times she'll take a step or two and fall back on her butt. And then there's that magic moment when two steps become three...then four... five... and before you know it, she's doing it. Stronger. More confident. Gone. Never looking back.

Now imagine if she had given in to those shaky little legs at first. She wouldn't be walking, running, jumping rope… do you get my point? We all start out something new on shaky legs. Yes, it would be easier just to stop, and maybe wait for someone to carry you. But at some point in this life, you'll have to pull yourself up and take step after step after step until what was once scary becomes steady.

And before you know it you are running—towards your best year, your best life, and your best you.

Maybe who we are isn't so much about what we do, but rather what we are capable of when we least expect it. – Jodi Picoult

#GoForIt 🔲🔲

How To Finish Your Race

Focus on the finish line: The worst thing you can do is take your eyes off of the finish line. Distractions will come. Noise from other people will infiltrate your positive thoughts in an effort to cause you to question what you've set out to do. Focus on the finish line. Stay clear and set on your dreams. Remain disciplined. Make the right moves for the right reasons at the right time. Focus. Focus. Focus.

Pick up your pace to complete your race: You will know if you are not moving at a pace suitable to meet your goals. If you are not reaching milestones soon enough, check your pace. It could be fear forcing you to slow down and question every move. If you feel behind, chances are you are. Check in with yourself regularly and push harder when you have to.

Pass the baton. When working with a partner or even someone who put their hand in the air to support you, know when it's time to pass something on. If you've done your part and it's their turn to run the race, let them. Don't worry about getting the accolades for your ability to pull it off alone. Allow the right people to support you when it's necessary. Their success is important too. You can all win.

ONE MORE THING...

Your best year ever starts today.

Your start may have been a little shakier than you expected. You may have lost something or someone. Your plans have come undone and you need to reset. Give yourself the grace to do that.

What does your best year look like? Write it out here.

_____

_____

_____

_____

Professional/Career/Business:

_____

_____

_____

_____

Health:

Finances:

Family/Personal:

Chapter 10
BEYOND YOU

Your purpose is so much bigger.

Throughout this book, we've spent a significant amount of time talking about you and the steps you can take to pull more out of your passion and your potential. The focus has been on you—your dreams, your goals, and the one thing (or maybe more) you really want to do. This is your journey and admittedly, the burden of the heavy lifting it will take to bring your dreams into fruition is on you.

It's for everyone else around you too.

But this is the thing—your purpose—is not all about you.

#GoForIt

You've been given something significant to share and that something is meant to come through you. It could be your story in a book. It could be stability for your community through a brick-and-mortar store in your neighborhood. It could be a new ministry in your church or a scholarship fund for young leaders. Whatever your something is, it is so much more than you. It will expand so much further than your hands. It will outweigh you, outreach you, and outdo you. The something—your thing—will be bigger, better, and higher than anything you could imagine.

This is why you have the responsibility, not the option, to show up.

Whether we like it or not, we are here to be an inspiration—a push—to other people. Someone, somewhere, is watching you and waiting for you to step into purpose. Their dreams are on hold. Their lives are not fulfilled. They are not the fullest or best representation of themselves because you are holding back.

What about the young woman at work who wants to step into a management role? She is watching *you*.

What about the person who wants to start her own business, but doesn't know where to start? *You* may be their example.

What about the person who is meant to help you build your dream in your company? They are waiting for *you*.

Show up.

You are someone's voice. You are someone's hope. You are a reminder of the strength someone didn't know they had. Yes you! You may be thinking, "How can I possibly be that to somebody I don't even know?" Think about who has been that for you. Did they know you were watching?

When you don't show up—

When you don't pursue your destiny like your life depends on it—

When you don't do the thing you are being called to do—

Someone else is stuck, waiting, wondering, wishing for an opportunity to move forward.

Your life was not lived for you—it was lived for someone else.

Show up.

Now, Go For It!

You've read this book and we hope you feel more empowered to go after what you want in this life. For every one of you, that means something different. You may want to start your own business or expand the one you have. You may want a promotion at work, to write a book, or be a better wife or mother this year.

Whatever your one thing is in this life, you can have it. The question is not can you have it or even if you can do it.

The question is: Will you do it?

Will you fight for what you want, even when it's hard?

Will you push past those obstacles?

Will you choose faith over fear?

Will you never give up?

Will you turn this year around and make it your best year ever?

When we met a few years ago, we had no idea what our lives would mean to each other. We didn't know how strong our bond of sisterhood would become. We didn't know how our journeys would intersect. We didn't know that each of our purposes would align so we would become ONE.

We had to be open to the possibilities for more than we could see or imagine.

And so here we are.

If you've learned nothing else from these pages, this life is full of possibilities. There is so much in the world waiting for you. Maybe you've already accomplished some, or all, of what you've set out to do years ago. You have the career or the business you desire. But what's next? How can you expand, be bigger, and live bolder? Even as we write this book, we're thinking about what's next for us, both together and as individuals. That's the thing, you never stop going. You never stop pushing for the next level or searching for that next big thing that God has for you to do.

Life is about growth, about taking risks, about faith in what you can't see. Life is about believing in your ability to achieve, to do what seems impossible, and to live your dreams—all of them. Don't stop simply because you've reached one goal. Set new ones, and make them bigger than the ones you've set before. And yes, you may be shaking in your boots, and that's okay. Use that fear to cement your faith. You'll need both along this journey, so take them by the hand and by all means, keep going.

Are you ready to live out your purpose?

Are you ready to lift the limits on your life and live fully?

Are you ready to chase—and catch—your dreams?

This is your time. You've been holding back. You've been living fearfully,

Let's look at where you are now. Through our lives and our stories, you realize now that obstacles are meant to overcome. When you feel like giving up, you can refer back to those chapters in the book for tips to renew your courage and faith. You've set big goals. You've released fear. You will begin to clear the clutter from your mind, your spirit, and your physical surroundings so you can open your life to the abundance and overflow that are waiting to pour into your life. Don't pause—push. Don't stop—go. Don't stay planted—grow. Focus on what matters most to you and define success on your own terms. And be extraordinary in the process.

You're in the right frame of mind to win.

Will this be easy? Absolutely not. But growth at the level you are seeking demands work. It will be hard. It will be challenging. There will be sweat and likely a few tears. But you can do this. You can go for it.

You will go for it.

If you are teetering on the edge of your dreams, our hope is that this book will push you to fly. You were created for something more, something extraordinary, and the choice to live that out is yours. Will you jump? Will you feel your fear and do it anyway? Will you get up and work hard, even when the obstacles are so big and so uncertain that the other side seems unreachable?

Here's the thing—that other side? It's your destiny. It's everything you've ever wanted or dreamed about. It's here, waiting for you to go for it, to choose. So what are you waiting for?

Today, we want you to...

See Your Obstacles as Opportunities

Never Give Up

And decide this will be your Best Year Ever!

NOTES

Chapter 1: Sometimes You Just Gotta Change The Tire

You are extraordinary and extraordinary takes heart. Test your courage with small wins and build on those. Call on your courage to replenish your faith and when faced with fear, recall those times when you overcame something impossible. Now do it again.

When it comes to success, you have to hunger for it more than you fear it. Remember the F.E.A.R. Principle.

#GoForIt 🔲🔲

Chapter 2: Play Anyway

Even if no one else shows up for you, you have to play anyway. **When it's time to play in this life, you may have to be your own cheerleader.** Be your own encourager and superhero. These are your dreams and you have to fight for them when no one else will. It's worth it for your destiny. Always be willing to work harder, run faster, jump higher and go further that everyone else.

#GoForIt 🔲🔲

Chapter 3: Be Willing To Put All Of Your Cards On The Table

Betting on yourself is worth every bit of the risk. There is no Plan B. You have to want success more than you want anything else. You have one shot. And never underestimate the power of passion and allow your passion to align you with your purpose.

#GoForIt 🔲🔲

Chapter 4: Behind Closed Doors

The doors to our dreams are to be opened. Try the key. Turn the knob. Knock. Find out what's waiting for you. When people try to close doors on you with negativity or an attempt to block you from an opportunity, refuse to give up. Keep knocking. Keep pushing. Close the door on self-doubt, comparison, and giving up too soon.

#GoForIt 🄵🄸

Chapter 5: Take the Leap

Fear will tell you there's something else you need before you can walk towards the dreams and the destiny that's calling you. Don't listen. Life is a series of leaps from one change, one goal, one success, to the next. Big leaps mean big rewards. Take those big leaps and don't underestimate your ability to fly. Find angels to support you along the way.

#GoForIt 🄵🄸

Chapter 6: Nothing To Lose

Following your passion and deciding to go for your dreams is a decision. Refuse to quit on your dreams. Quitting is only delaying your destiny. Stay the course. Keep your vison in front of you at all times as a reminder to never give up on yourself.

#GoForIt 🄵🄸

Chapter 7: Let Go of Yesterday

There is a new season waiting for you once you've made the room to receive it. Look around you and decide what needs to go. It's time for you to grow. To receive the new, you must relinquish the old. Clear the clutter from your life and always be willing to release what is no longer necessary in this season of your life. You cannot hold old and new at the same time—make room.

Take control of your life and your next steps. You can change your circumstances today.

#GoForIt

Chapter 8: Under Reconstruction

Ride out your storms. Reconstruct your life. Fight for what belongs to you—everything you've been promised, dreamed about, and worked for. Don't be afraid to rebuild.

#GoForIt

Chapter 9: It's How You Finish, Not How You Start

Fight past your willingness to throw your hands up when you don't start strong. Setbacks don't mean stop—they mean pause, change course, and keep going. You can still make this year your best year ever. Now is the time to pick up your pace and run your race. Stay focused and call on your partners and team when you need to.

#GoForIt

Chapter 10: Beyond You

But this is the thing—your purpose—is not all about you. Your purpose is so much bigger than you realize. There are people who can't step into their positon until you show up. Your life was not lived for you—it was lived for someone else. Be the inspiration and the power they need. Someone is waiting.

#GoForIt

QUOTES

Chapter 1

Every Obstacle Is Just A Stepping Stone To Your Greatness. – Constance Carter #GoForIt 🔲🔲

I Can't Expect God To Bless Me With The Great Things If I Am Not Willing To Do The Little Things. - Constance Carter #GoForIt 🔲🔲

If You Want Something, Go Get It. Period. - Chris Gardner #GoForIt 🔲🔲

Everything You Want Is On The Other Side Of Fear- Jack Canfield #GoForIt 🔲🔲

Chapter 2

It's Your Road, And Yours Alone. Others May Walk It With You But No One Can Walk It For You. – Rumi #GoForIt 🔲🔲

You Will Never Rise Above The Level At Which You See Yourself- Constance Carter #GoForIt 🔲🔲

Chapter 3

I wanted success as much as I wanted to live. – Constance Carter #GoForIt 🔲🔲

If you are willing to do what's easy, life will be hard. But if you are willing to do what's hard, life will be easy. - T. Harv Ecker #GoForIt 🔲🔲

You can only become truly accomplished at something you love. Don't make money your goal. Instead, pursue the things you love doing, and do them so well that people can't take their eyes off you. – Maya Angelou #GoForIt 🔲🔲

Success leaves clues. – Tony Robbins #GoForIt 🔲🔲

Chapter 4

Two things you never get to do—quit and give up. – Tinarsha Brown **#GoForIt** 🔲🔲

Don't give up. Normally it is the last key on the ring which opens the door. – Paulo Coelho **#GoForIt** 🔲🔲

Courage doesn't always roar. Sometimes courage is the quiet voice at the end of the day saying, "I'll try again tomorrow. —Maryanne Radmacher **#GoForIt** 🔲🔲

Failing is a part of success. You have to fall down to get back up. – Tinarsha Brown **#GoForIt** 🔲🔲

Chapter 5

Now faith is confidence in what we hope for and assurance about what we do not see. —Hebrews 11:1 **#GoForIt** 🔲🔲

Dreams are necessary to life. – Anais Nin **#GoForIt** 🔲🔲

Destiny flocks together. – T.D. Jakes **#GoForIt** 🔲🔲

If you quit—quitting will become easier and easier for the rest of your life. – Osman Minkara **#GoForIt** 🔲🔲

Chapter 6

If you quit—quitting will become easier and easier for the rest of your life. – Osman Minkara **#GoForIt** 🔲🔲

"Don't let your fear hold your passion hostage, you have nothing to lose once you release the fear" - Tinarsha Brown **#GoForIt** 🔲🔲

Chapter 7

And no one puts new wine into old wineskins. For the wine would burst the wineskins, and the wine and the skins would both be lost. New wine calls for new wineskins. – Mark 2:22 #GoForIt 🔵🟢

There are good things waiting to manifest for you. But you have to be willing to let go. – Sheila Green #GoForIt 🔵🟢

Fear and familiarity will keep you stuck. – Sheila Green #GoForIt 🔵🟢

You will never get what you deserve if you won't let go of what you already have. – Sheila Green #GoForIt 🔵🟢

Chapter 8

I am going to make tomorrow a good day. For me. – Sheila Green #GoForIt 🔵🟢

Rock bottom became the solid foundation on which I rebuilt my life. – J.K. Rowling #GoForIt 🔵🟢

If you just keep breathing, you cannot be conquered. – Oprah Winfrey #GoForIt 🔵🟢

Chapter 9

Maybe who we are isn't so much about what we do, but rather what we are capable of when we least expect it. – Jodi Picoult #GoForIt 🔵🟢

Chapter 10

There is no greater gift you can give or receive than to honor your calling. It's why you were born. And how you become most truly alive. – Oprah Winfrey #GoForIt 🔵🟢

MORE QUOTES TO LIVE BY

QUOTES ON PURPOSE

If you can't figure out your purpose, figure out your passion. For your passion will lead you right to your purpose. – T.D. Jakes **#GoForIt** ■◎

The heart of human excellence often begins to beat when you discover a pursuit that absorbs you, frees you, challenges you, or gives you a sense of meaning, joy, or passion. – Terry Orlick **#GoForIt** ■◎

And no heart has ever suffered when it goes in search of its dream. – Paulo Coelho **#GoForIt** ■◎

You've got to be willing to lose everything to gain yourself. – Iyanla Vanzant **#GoForIt** ■◎

QUOTES ON DREAMS

You can't just sit there and wait for people to give you that golden dream, you've got to get out there and make it happen for yourself. – Diana Ross **#GoForIt** ■◎

Notice when your heart leaps up in joyous exuberance... In these moments the voice of your spirit is speaking directly to you. – Justine Willis Toms **#GoForIt** ■◎

Dreams express what your soul is telling you, so as crazy as your dream might seem, you have to let that out. – Eleni Gabre- Madhin **#GoForIt** ■◎

You have to speak your dreams out loud. – Kelly Corrigan **#GoForIt** ■◎

How can you know what you are capable of if you don't embrace the unknown? – Esmeralda Santiago **#GoForIt** ■◎

QUOTES ON STRENGTH

People underestimate their capacity to change. There is never a right time to a do a difficult thing. - *John Porter* #GoForIt 🔵🔵

Each of us guards a gate of change that can only be unlocked from the inside. – *Marilyn Ferguson* #GoForIt 🔵🔵

The real winners in life are the people who look at every situation with an expectation that they can make it work for the better. – *Barbara Pletcher* #GoForIt 🔵🔵

MEET THE AUTHOR: CONSTANCE CARTER

When a woman's very essence is extraordinary, she influences everyone in her midst to relentlessly seek their own success.

She takes on business and life with a knowing that she was bred to achieve, greatly.

She fiercely challenges every barrier she encounters, refusing to yield until the obstacle bows into its rightful place as another opportunity.

She is Constance Carter.

From birth, Constance was told that she could be and do anything she dreamed or desired. With that ideal imprinted on her soul, she went out into the world always willing to bet on herself—and refusing to relinquish until she won.

Today, she is wife, mother, author, bass player, investor, motivational speaker and CEO, a renaissance woman in every sense of the word.

After obtaining her real estate license in 2002, followed by her broker's license in 2006, Constance lent her brilliance as a sales leader to several notable agencies. Quickly ascending to seven-figure producer status, her transaction portfolio boasts an estimated $200 million and at first competed with, and then crushed, that of her peers. During that time, Constance did what every visionary does—

dreamed a bigger dream for herself and the industry at large. She set her sights on establishing her own real estate brokerage and a business that authentically reflected her core values of holistic service and success. She envisioned a company that was not just *in* the community, but *of* the community—one that helped, educated and transformed.

And in 2010, Catalyst Real Estate Professionals was born.

She started Catalyst as a boutique real estate company, and the firm quickly ascended to one of the top real estate firms in California's Central Valley. With agents throughout Northern California, Constance is shifting the real estate industry from one that is driven solely by the transaction and led more by transformation. She is deeply devoted to helping as many people as possible to achieve the American dream of homeownership and will allow nothing to stand between them and their wealth-building goals. When she found faltering credit scores to be an obstacle many clients struggled to overcome, she delved into the topic, mastered it and garnered her Credit Expert Certification. Constance penned her expertise in a book, *Keeping Score: What You Need to Know to Make Your Credit Score Grow*, empowering people with the knowledge to shift the trajectory of their financial futures.

With a passionate emphasis on hardworking Americans, Constance is leading the charge to educate aspiring homeowners about the opportunities for creating generational wealth through real estate. Along with her team of agents, who are as committed to the mission as she, Constance will forge a new path for success, one that is legacy-driven and rooted in reaching back to give while climbing the ladder to greatness.

Constance believes, emphatically, that anyone can do anything they set their minds to—if they are willing to harness the drive it takes to go for it. As a rising speaker and author, she has a motivational message for business leaders, urging them to uncover their own resilience and to find power in her personal story and a blueprint in her success.

An overcomer in every sense of the word, there is not an obstacle she will not face—and then conquer.

There is not a heart she will not inspire.

There is not a person in her presence that she will not propel forward into dreams more vivid, more vast, than they ever thought possible.

Because, after all, that is what extraordinary women do.

MEET THE AUTHOR: TINARSHA BROWN

There are people who cringe at the word *no*—and then there are those who are charged by it.

There are people who when confronted with a closed door, pause—and then there are those who are empowered to burst through.

There are people who accept others' meaning of success—and there are those who define their own.

Meet Tinarsha Brown.

A true trailblazer in the real estate industry, Tinarsha began her entrepreneurial journey in 2002. Following the footprint of her mother, a top-selling, multi-million dollar producer, she was fueled by naysayers who audaciously questioned her birthright to excellence. Charting her own destiny, she garnered her residential real estate license and within three years of a faithful leap into a full-time career in 2005, she not only dismissed the resounding *no* —she demolished it. Quickly surpassing the six-figure mark, Tinarsha ascended as an industry leader, earning the coveted Rookie of the Year Award and numerous other accolades and applause along the way. And the honors simply kept coming.

If you ask Tinarsha, or any of her peers, where her brilliance lies, it is unquestionably in the art of the deal. She is masterful at every nuance of negotiation, with a boldness befitting of the mogul she is. At any table, she conquers with an ease and a power that is unmatched. To date, her portfolio boasts over 250 million in volume and she's still counting.

Once she cemented her own success, Tinarsha knew she had to reach back and help other aspiring agents to find their own. She envisioned a firm that created a path paved with opportunities for both her team and families to build legacies and generational wealth. Her vision became a reality in 2014 when Tinarsha opened the doors to her six-figure real estate brokerage, Intero Real Estate. Yet again, she answered her calling to be more for not only herself, but for those she has been purposed to lead. She stands for her agents every day—championing their right to succeed, advocating for their possibilities and inspiring them to their next level of greatness. Dedicated to her mother, her company is one of the leading residential real estate firms in the San Francisco Bay Area, and will be legendary in the industry for the dollars it reaps, but more so for the seeds of difference it sows in the community and in lives.

Tinarsha's acclaimed success as an entrepreneur and business leader is just the first chapter of her legacy. As a motivational speaker and an author, she shares her testimony of unbreakable will, undeniable passion and unabashed faith from stages nationwide so that youth, women and aspiring business leaders can hear her heart, glean from her strength and be changed.

Yes—she is tenacious.

Yes—she beat the odds.

And yes—she fearlessly stepped off the edge of a cliff—and found her wings in flight.

But truly?

She is a woman who simply never gave up.

MEET THE AUTHOR: SHEILA GREEN

A woman with soul for service, a desire for greatness and an intrinsic drive for success anchors the world.

She is a wealth builder who redefines prosperity not by more money—but by the lasting impact she makes when she uplifts her community.

She is a consummate strategist who sees opportunities for growth and harnesses the commitment necessary to move ideas forward.

She is a futurist with a vision for tomorrow that is so vivid, so vibrant, that even your best yesterday pales in comparison.

Meet Sheila Greene.

Highly regarded in real estate and in business for pioneering innovation, Sheila has the fearlessness to be first. She cultivated her competitive spirit as young athlete, but her performance was never driven by a desire to stand in the spotlight alone. She dominated the court and track, always patiently awaiting that inevitable moment when her mastery would be the difference. Whenever her team needs her, Sheila does what champions do—she shows up. And it is that sentiment—that devotion—that fuels her, and she unselfishly shows up, again and again, willing to carry a team on her shoulders, never faltering.

She is destined to elicit change—in people, in business and in the world. A big-picture thinker, her vision is always 10,000 feet above what exists. She has an insightfulness that accelerates every moment past what is and into the realm of what can be. She is genius at discovering the possibilities in people, pulling the best out of them and showing them who they can be—even before they see themselves.

Powered by a passion to see people win, Sheila helps others to imagine their future—one rich with possibilities and significance. In 2012, she launched her innovative sports consultancy, Elite Prospect Zone, Inc., in response to the increasing number of student athletes whose educational performance did not align with their phenomenal potential. Within a span of two years, every player on her inaugural client roster was offered a full scholarship from a four-year university. This woman changes the game in every sense of the word.

Sheila has an uncompromising strength that doesn't wane during the journey—no matter how uncertain the path. Her 2015 began with one tumultuous event after another, including a devastating health diagnosis. Yet she was steadfast in her claim that she would emerge victorious. And so she did. True to character and grounded in her faith, she molded her broken pieces into a breakthrough, shattering profit records and solidifying her purpose to be a courageous voice for anyone staring adversity in the face and questioning their ability to win. She will push you towards your destiny, and then dare you *not* to go get it.

And she is undoubtedly on the cusp of her next best year.

It's one you will not want to miss.

47164037R00075

Made in the USA
San Bernardino, CA
24 March 2017